Back to Basics

Francis Schrag

Back to Basics

Fundamental Educational
Questions Reexamined

Jossey-Bass Publishers • San Francisco

Substantial discounts on bulk quantities of Jossey-Bass books are available to corporations, professional associations, and other organizations. For details and discount information, contact the special sales department at Jossey-Bass Inc., Publishers. (415) 433-1740; Fax (415) 433-0499.

For international orders, please contact your local Paramount Publishing International office.

TCF Manufactured in the United States of America on Lyons Falls Pathfinder Tradebook. This paper is acid-free and 100 percent totally chlorine-free.

The epigraph on p. xv is from John Dewey's *Experience and Education* (1938), reprinted by permission of *Kappa Delta Pi*, an International Honor Society in Education.

Library of Congress Cataloging-in-Publication Data

Schrag, Francis.
    Back to basics : fundamental educational questions reexamined / Francis Schrag. — 1st ed.
        p.   cm. — (The Jossey-Bass education series)
    Includes bibliographical references and index.
    ISBN 0-7879-0060-5
    1. Education—United States—Philosophy. 2. Education—United States—Aims and objectives. I. Title. II. Series.
LB14.7.S37   1995
370'.973—dc20   94-24346
                                                                      CIP

FIRST EDITION
HB Printing   10 9 8 7 6 5 4 3 2 1   *Code 9513*

The Jossey-Bass Education Series

For Sally, who had faith in this project from the beginning.

Contents

Preface

"What's a philosopher of education good for, if not to help people think about education in a deeper and clearer way than they otherwise would?" my nonacademic friends and family members have often asked. It took me many years to acknowledge that they were right in asking the question. Even when I recognized the importance of the question, I had doubts about whether I could write the book I felt needed to be written. Had all those years in university classrooms criticizing others' texts while being loath to advance my own opinion left me with anything of my own to say? Could I say it in a way that was clear and readable? A sabbatical semester from the University of Wisconsin, Madison, and two months of summer funding from its graduate school gave me an opportunity to find out.

This book is the result. My title refers not to the three R's, but to the most basic educational questions our society, indeed any society, must grapple with. These fundamental questions have been asked and answered so many times before, though, that complete novelty of ideas would elude even the most original writer. My own thinking about education has its inspiration in John Dewey's mature writings on the topic, but I have borrowed only some of his ideas; others have been discarded to suit my own purposes and our own time and place. *Back to Basics* presupposes no background in either philosophy in general or Dewey's ideas in particular. I hope it reads neither like a conventional textbook nor like a work designed to impress learned colleagues at tenure time.

As I completed chapter drafts, I circulated them to friends and colleagues to get reactions and suggestions. Here I'd like to thank all those who helped me improve a sentence, a line of argument, or a chapter, including Rima Apple, David Benatar, Walter Feinberg, Adam Gamaron, Irwin Goldman, Karen Goldman, Jurgen Herbst, Carl Kaestle, Herb Kliebard, Mary Metz, Fred Newmann, Chris Ogren, Michael Olneck, Daniel Pekarsky, Andy Porter, Mary Sarko, Howard Temin, and Lew Zipin. Jim Carl, a graduate assistant, read the entire manuscript and provided many constructive suggestions. My friend Richard Merelman gave me invaluable guidance upon reading the first draft of the first chapter. When the entire manuscript was completed, his critical reading alerted me to difficulties confronting my argument that I've had a chance to try to remedy prior to publication. Two reviewers commissioned by Jossey-Bass gave a variety of useful suggestions that I've tried to incorporate in the book. Arthur Wirth was one; the second preferred to remain anonymous. David Wakeley helped me proofread. Finally, my wife, Sally, proved once again to be my best editor, and I'm grateful for her support during the year that I was immersed in this project.

Madison, Wisconsin   Francis Schrag
December 1994

Back to Basics

Perhaps the greatest of all pedagogical fallacies is the notion that a person learns only the particular thing he's studying at the time. Collateral learning in the way of formation of enduring attitudes, of likes and dislikes, may be and often is much more important than the spelling lesson or lesson in geography or history that is learned. For these attitudes are fundamentally what count in the future. The most important attitude that can be formed is that of desire to go on learning. If impetus in this direction is weakened instead of being intensified, something much more than mere lack of preparation takes place. The pupil is actually robbed of native capacities which otherwise would enable him to cope with the circumstances that he meets in the course of his life.

—John Dewey, 1938, pp. 49–50

Chapter One

Why Philosophy?

Phonics or whole language, a national curriculum or a voucher system, parent control or teacher autonomy, desegregation or academies for black males—amid the clamor of competing proposals, the voice of the philosopher is nowhere to be heard; it is missing from the conversation about the future of schooling. Jumping on one bandwagon after another, substituting sloganeering for sustained thinking, focusing on specifics without having a well-thought-through idea of what one is ultimately trying to accomplish—these tendencies can be seen as reflecting a certain superficiality in popular thinking and writing about education.

What might philosophy have to offer? Because of its focus on fundamental ideas, philosophy may not be well suited to coming up with blueprints for reform, but it is adept at deepening and sharpening the way we think about what schools can and should do. Philosophers concentrate on asking fundamental questions and try to defend them by means of persuasive argumentation. In framing their answers, philosophers try to capture what is essential about a phenomenon, doing justice to each of its important aspects without getting bogged down in details. When it comes to education, philosophers ask general questions about the proper aims of education, the most reasonable basis for selecting what students ought to study, and the way in which and the extent to which schools ought to be responsive to demands from the broader society, among many other topics. Philosophers of education see as their primary mission posing and answering the most basic questions. Some of these questions appear to have obvious answers—for example, why should we have public schools at all?—until we start thinking about them. Trying to defend answers that seem so obvious to many can be surprisingly difficult.

Back to Basics, then, is an inquiry into these fundamental educational questions. Its primary aim is not to formulate or defend particular policy initiatives but to examine the perspective from which such initiatives are viewed. The book is divided into nine chapters; Chapters Two through Eight each focus on a single question: What should our educational aspirations be? What should be taught in school? What is the nature of teaching and how can teaching be improved? How shall educators be held accountable for what they do or fail to do? Who should have ultimate authority in education? How should educators deal with social inequalities? Why is it so hard to reform schools? In the course of asking these questions, I examine our most basic beliefs about education, but since I can't examine them all simultaneously I accept, for argument's sake, certain assumptions in one chapter that I examine rigorously in another. In Chapter Two, for example, I assume that schools should continue to exist, and that their primary focus should be developing the intellect. Yet the existence of schools and the focus on intellectual development themselves need justification, and those topics are taken up in Chapter Three. To take another example, Chapters Two through Six give little acknowledgment to the problem of schooling in a very unequal society, but this problem becomes the exclusive issue in Chapter Seven.

My overall point of view as I've already admitted, is strongly influenced by my reading of John Dewey. How can I justify this in light of the widespread sentiment that Dewey is the source of our schools' problems rather than the source of their solutions? It's important to realize that, contrary to what is commonly assumed, Dewey actually had very little influence on American public schools.[1] Consider some of the charges against him: American schools focus on social frills rather than on academic essentials; they fail to value intellectual excellence or hard work; they invite irresponsibility in teachers and lack of civility in students. I challenge readers to find a single work of Dewey's that advocates any of these tendencies. How ironic, then, that at the very time Dewey is being blamed for most of the defects of American schools, winning proposals for many of the so-called "break-the-mold" schools funded in response to an initiative taken by President George Bush in 1991 bear the unmistakable stamp of his educational theory.[2] I can't think of more convincing evidence that existing public school classrooms bear little resemblance to Dewey's educational vision.

My argument in Chapter Two, on which the rest of the book depends, can be read as an extension and interpretation of the paragraph from Dewey's *Experience and Education* cited at the beginning of the book. But neither that chapter nor the rest of the book is intended to be a review or restatement of Dewey's philosophy of education. I would be disloyal to what Dewey said if I were merely to echo him without considering the new problems that have emerged and without considering the evidence that has accumulated since he stopped writing about education close to fifty years ago. Ignoring evidence is the one thing no admirer of Dewey would want to be accused of.

The skeptic might ask, "Do policy-minded citizens or educators concerned about school reform need to get involved in the philosophy of education?" We could answer no, especially if traditional patterns of activity are simply followed or blindly rejected without being given much thought. Here it is easy to fool ourselves, though. Even the most familiar patterns reinforce some values and derogate others; hence, they embody distinctive ideas and commitments, whether we are aware of this or not. Let me illustrate.

I sometimes begin my course in the philosophy of education by asking students to imagine that they have just been hired to teach second grade and they are about to set up their classroom for the first time. I ask them to sketch the way they would want the children's and teacher's desks laid out in the room. Some arrange the second-grade students in rows with the teacher in the front, some put the children in small groups with the teacher at the rear, and still others arrange all the desks in a large circle. I then point out that each arrangement carries with it a different set of ideas about how children are likely to behave, how they learn, and what the role of the teacher is supposed to be. If a teacher is placed in the front of the room, that is because one probably believes that her main jobs are keeping order and imparting knowledge. If a teacher is placed at the rear of the room, one probably believes that her main job is monitoring learning activities that the children can engage in by themselves individually or in small groups. At this point one of my students will often say: "Okay, I see that these room arrangements represent different educational ideals, but we don't need philosophers to evaluate them. Educational researchers could design an experiment to settle the question of which is best, couldn't they?"

The questioner has a point, but the experiment will only be persuasive if we can first agree on how we might ascertain which classroom is the most successful, and that's only possible if we share the same definition or idea of educational success. Reading through a range of newspaper or magazine articles on education, we can readily see that we don't, in fact, agree about that at all. Before we can conduct any experiments, we need to decide on what schools should do for children. No amount of educational research will provide an answer to that question. Most researchers will, in fact, be happy to turn it over to philosophers. Since so much ultimately depends on the answer to this question, it makes an ideal starting point for my inquiry.

Chapter Two

Aspirations

What do we want schools to do for children? My own answer will emerge more clearly against the backdrop of prevailing alternatives. Most contemporary writers identify the transmission of knowledge as the primary purpose of schooling. For some, such as David Kearns and Denis Doyle, the specification of what needs to be known depends on the requirements of the workplace in the international competition for economic ascendancy. Among those who find an educational vision focused on the demands of the workplace limiting, some, like E. D. Hirsch, Jr., and Chester Finn, Jr., contend that what contemporary schools most neglect is the transmission of factual knowledge. For Hirsch the principal facts are the cultural references needed to understand articles in the *New York Times,* the *Washington Post,* and similar publications. Finn alleges that the important facts were taught to our parents (or grandparents) before the misguided views of progressive educators took over American public schools. Other educational critics such as neoconservative William Bennett identify what needs to be learned primarily with knowledge found in certain texts deemed central to our civilization. Finally, some, like Howard Gardner, describe what needs to be learned in terms of the conceptual knowledge of the world provided by the various intellectual disciplines.[1]

For yet another group of educational reformers, simply identifying what children ought to *know* is not sufficient. The answer to the question of what schools ought to aim at must be formulated in terms of what proficiencies students can demonstrate. According to this view, represented, for example, by William Spady, originator of the currently popular Outcome-Based Education, it is what students are actually *able to do* that counts, not the understanding they have in their heads.[2] Moreover, exponents of this position will say, if we are clear about what we specifically want young people to be able to do, we will be well on our way to evaluating the success of their schooling, because it is not nearly as hard to find out what things people can demonstrate as it is to find out what they understand.

I think it fair to say that despite significant differences between them, all the authors mentioned so far distance themselves from what they take to be John Dewey's views and contributions to American education. Since my position is directly descended from that of Dewey, it is not surprising that I disagree with them all.

I believe that we should reject both the formulation that emphasizes what students should know and the formulation that emphasizes what they can demonstrate. Why? What people know and are able to do at age eighteen is important, but because we can anticipate neither the problems they will face nor the resources they will have available to solve them, these are not the most important lessons they will have learned in school. Isn't our adult concern with the next generation ultimately a concern with the kind of people they will *be* and with what they will or will not *do?* What finally determines people's character and their actions is not what they could demonstrate at some earlier point or what they once understood, but what they can learn to do, what they're disposed to do, and what they care about.

The discussion so far is abstract; let's make it concrete. Suppose that you took a nutrition class at some point in your schooling. You would have acquired information, such as what foods belong to various food groups, and you would have developed skills, such as the ability to read and interpret the labels found in the supermarket, but you could have excelled in the course and still eat badly, by eating foods you know you shouldn't, eating too much or too little, or failing to profit from new nutritional information. Ultimately what and how you eat is determined by the attitude you take toward nutrition and toward the health of your own body and by your ability to profit from new information. These attitudes and that ability are what determine the use, if any, you will make of the information you learned in the nutrition class. Undoubtedly, you have now forgotten some of what was taught. Indeed, much of the information you were taught is likely to be invalidated by current evidence, but if you can interpret newer information, if you care about eating well, these deficiencies can be remedied. On the other hand, all the facts and skills you learned in the class will have been to no avail if you don't give a hoot about your health.

Now suppose that the only literature class you took in high school was American literature. No doubt you learned many facts about authors, characters, and literary styles and developed skills such as the ability to decipher figures of speech in poetry and understand the author's point of view. You may have achieved a high grade in the course. Should your teacher feel fully satisfied with your success? Not necessarily. Perhaps you never pick up serious novels or poems for enjoyment or personal enrichment, your taste in magazines runs to trashy novels and magazines, you never want to spend money to see a serious drama or even a movie based on a classic play or novel—in short, your reading and entertainment habits are no different from the habits of those who never had a course like yours. We might legitimately consider your literary education a failure.

One reason for my emphasis on dispositions, habits of mind, intellectual virtues, character traits, "enduring attitudes," to use Dewey's phrase—the terminology is not important—and on the capacity to learn is that so much of the material we learn in school is forgotten. How many of us could still solve the chemistry or algebra problems we once mastered? How many could translate a paragraph of Caesar's Latin into English? How many could still write an informative essay about *The Red Badge of Courage* or the unification of Italy? Some who would fail such exercises—I count myself among them—were successful students and a few, like myself, made the pursuit of learning their vocation. We all recall some stray details from our school days—a poem we had to recite in grade school, a formula for finding the distance traveled by a falling object—and, of course, some people retain a good deal more of what they learned in school. I daresay, however, that Robert Kelly's recollection of his calculus class (in this case, a college class) is typical. Now a poet and teacher of writing, Kelly recalls:

> The professor who taught us calculus in the required yearlong course had a quirky way of opening a pack of cigarettes. With his strong, sharp, tan-stained thumbnail, he would first score, then slice, the front of the pack from top to bottom, right through the camel, so that, pried back a bit, the paper wrapper would gape like a purse and show the cigarettes inside. From these he would select his smoke with some delicacy.
>
> And that's what I know of calculus. . . . Greek letters and all those mysterious quantities approaching zero fade, and I see a weary, lanky, dusty man doing something weird with cigarettes while his eyes look for something, anything, out of the window high over Harlem.[3]

The porousness of human memory is undeniable, especially for facts and ideas learned in school; this porousness, itself, appears, unfortunately, to be one of those things all too easily forgotten by those who write about schooling. Fortunately or unfortunately, not everything that we develop in school is lost. It is not the facts or the skills, but the "enduring attitudes" toward learning, the habits of mind, that stick and become part of us.

Three Key Aspirations

Let it be granted that what we can learn, what we're disposed to do, and what we care about are of ultimate importance. Where does that take us? Aren't there an inordinate number of things, from food for the body to food for the soul, that people should care about, and a virtually infinite list of activities they should be disposed to engage in? More important, don't people disagree about what it is important to care about? And, finally, can the school be held responsible for the attitudes of its graduates, attitudes that derive from so many different sources? Let's try to deal with the first two questions first.

Given that there are so many things you and I think the young should learn to care about and given that the two of us are likely to disagree on what they are, what we need is a way to distill all these specifics into a few general concerns whose importance will be recognized by everyone. I believe there is such a way.

Let's try a thought experiment modeled on that of the noted philosopher John Rawls.[4] Imagine that you and I and a large number of American adults reflecting very diverse points of view and stations in life are meeting to prescribe principles for the education of our great-grandchildren. Suppose now (this isn't hard to imagine) that we are unable to describe the precise contours of the society our great-grandchildren will inhabit or their particular place in that society. Finally, suppose we agree at the outset that our focus is to be the intellectual development of the young, broadly interpreted. (This assumption will be examined in Chapter Three.) We are charged with the task of identifying the most essential things that we want our great-grandchildren to learn. We would want this from them no matter what part of society they come from or are destined for, no matter what their native endowment, no matter what the particular tastes and values of their parents, and no matter whether they will be educated in conventional schools, at home, or in institutions that have not yet been invented.

What would this thought experiment have to say to us here and now as we ponder ways to improve schools attended by our own children and our neighbors' children? The point of locating the thought experiment in the future is this: we don't want our answer to the question, What should schools do for children? to be biased by our particular place in society or by our own or our children's distinctive tastes, talents, and attitudes; nor will we achieve the perspective we need if our answers are colored too strongly by today's newspaper headlines or television accounts. On the other hand, by focusing on our own great-grandchildren rather than on anonymous children in the next century, we concern ourselves with individuals in whose prospects we feel a stake.

I believe that we, their great-grandparents, could agree on three key aspirations (I use *aspiration* rather than *goal* because the latter connotes a specific destination that either is or isn't reached, a connotation I deplore):

1. Our great-grandchildren should care about arguments and evidence bearing on any course of action or conclusion they are contemplating.
2. They should be disposed to continue their own learning.
3. To the extent possible, they should have developed the capacity to continue that learning.

Why would we agree that these three aspirations are essential? Let me try to defend each one in order. But first, what do I mean by saying that our great-grandchildren should learn to *care* about arguments and evidence? Caring can't be reduced to a set of specific behaviors, but people who care about evidence and argument seek to find out the facts and to discover what's at stake in the decisions facing them. They listen to or read what partisans of a variety of points of view have to say. Most important, they are willing to consider evidence, even when it challenges the doctrines they're most comfortable with. It is hard for us to anticipate the precise challenges our great-grandchildren will face, but we have no reason to think they will be easier than those we have faced. Few of us believe that we can face our own challenges without being able to hear or read what others have thought or found out about a subject. Refusing to seek evidence and attempting to deny evidence we've been confronted with are dubious strategies, whether in our personal or our collective lives. All of us would realize that our great-grandchildren's decisions are likely to be better ones if they care about what the evidence shows concerning an issue or problem.

Taking up the second aspiration, it is inconceivable that any of us would find tolerable the prospect that our great-grand-

children's curiosity about the world and themselves had been stifled as the result of their school experience. Regardless of their distinctive capabilities or personal goals, the disposition to keep
on learning will be indispensable. Finally, the disposition to
continue learning would be without value if the capacity to engage
in that learning were not developed. Most human beings are born
not just with a boundless natural curiosity but with a magnificent
capacity to satisfy that curiosity, one that even the most sophisticated computer can't duplicate. (There is, of course, little reason
to think that this capacity is the same for all of us in all areas.)
Since we have no way of knowing whether our great-grandchildren will want to learn dance, mathematics, Japanese language or
ceramics, farming, computer programming, or all of those, we can
only hope that their educational institutions will develop their natural capabilities for learning in a variety of fields.

Clarifications

Knowing what we do about our own children and the schools they
attend, other aspirations may loom larger for us here and now than
the three I have identified, but I believe that these three have as
close to a universal claim to our support as any that could be formulated. Remember that the thought experiment focused on great-
grandchildren was only a device to help us answer the general
question of what *our* educational aspirations ought to be. Whatever
else they aim at, our schools should aspire to the following: that
their students become committed to reaching conclusions about
what to think or do with due respect for the arguments and evidence available, and that they retain both a desire and a capacity
to keep on learning. Any educational program or institution that
subverts these aspirations must be judged a failure, whatever else it
accomplishes.

"Does this imply," the reader may ask, "that teachers or principals ought to set these as their *explicit* aims? Are teachers no longer
to teach students how to add fractions or to understand the causes

of World War I? Are students to develop concern about matters of which they have no understanding? Can one develop the disposition or the capacity to keep on learning without having learned anything in particular? Can one learn to respect evidence in general? Isn't the kind of evidence needed to weigh an aesthetic judgment different from that needed to reach a conclusion in the sciences, for example?"

The questioner is right in suggesting that commitment presupposes understanding, as well as in suggesting that there is no such thing as generic learning; all learning involves gaining knowledge about something specific like how to add fractions or how to understand the events leading up to the First World War. Moreover, I do not deny that what counts as appropriate evidence and how we seek and weigh it will vary with the subject matter and the kind of question being considered. These cannot be learned except insofar as the student becomes acquainted with the distinctive ways of thinking and judging that are available in diverse fields of inquiry.

The point I insist on is only this: when thinking about or engaging in educational activities, we should not lose sight of what ultimately matters, which is not whether the students in history class can pass Friday's test on the causes of the war, but on whether they develop a taste and appreciation for the study of how things got to be the way they are, whether they develop a capacity to understand and interpret documents written at other times and in other places, and whether they develop a sense of themselves as successful learners. If the immediate objective is gained at the expense of the ultimate, the victory is hollow.

My three key educational aspirations should play a role somewhat like the one that happiness ought to play in our personal lives. Our focus is always on satisfactions to be had from particular choices—taking this job, meeting that friend, participating in that activity, and so on—but if we seek happiness rather than momentary pleasure, we have to think of the long term and the larger pattern our particular choices make. Like happiness, love, and mutual understanding, all things we cherish, success in realizing the three educational aspirations will be difficult to assess and impossible to measure. But in education as in life, the *worthiness* of an aspiration is one thing; the ease or difficulty of assessing how close we come to achieving it is a quite different one. We cannot dodge the issue of accountability and will take it up in a later chapter, but we also cannot allow our aspirations to be held hostage to demands for accountability, no matter how well intentioned.

We still haven't addressed our third question, how the school can be held responsible for attitudes stemming from so many sources. Even in the intellectual sphere, the school is only a single influence on what people will ultimately care about and be disposed to do. Let us imagine a social studies teacher responding to my three key aspirations like this: "It is not my responsibility to sustain students' desire to learn or to get them to care about the evidence bearing on interpretations of the First World War or on any other question; my job is only to teach them what events led up to the First World War, what the turning points of the war were, and what its consequences were, period. If they know that, I've succeeded. If not, not. That job is hard enough, but at least it's a job I can try to accomplish."

Of course I sympathize with the burdens that this teacher already feels and have no wish to add to her distress. But I do not accept her thinking about her responsibilities, which she underestimates in some respects and overestimates in others. Whether she accepts the responsibility or not, it is clear by the way she interacts with the students, by the attitude she exhibits toward the subject matter, by the kinds of questions and assignments she poses, by the satisfactions and dissatisfactions she evinces, and by the rewards and penalties she metes out that she influences the *attitudes* her students will adopt toward history, toward the importance of evidence bearing on conclusions, and even toward school learning itself.

We have charged the teacher with the task of promoting her students' intellectual development, but we must recognize that she is not uniquely responsible for the intellectual attitudes and dispositions her students develop. But then, neither is she uniquely responsible for what her students know or are able to do on her social studies test. Why not? Any student's performance on a school test will be the result of an enormous number of factors, most of which the school has little control over: resources and attitudes in the home that do or don't mesh with and reinforce those of the school, the attitudes of peers, or the impact of the media, inherited talents, handicaps, and proclivities, to name the most obvious.

A student who is asked to analyze the causes of the First World War might be thought to be drawing only on what he has learned in his social studies class, but that is an illusion. Of course, some (though perhaps not all) of the specific information he brings to the test on that topic may come from his social studies teacher or his textbook, but his ability to take notes on the important points and to recall them, to organize the relevant information in his mind before beginning to write, to express himself with a greater or lesser degree of coherence, correctness and conciseness, and elegance— all of these capabilities have been developed over many years and derive from many influences both in and outside the school. Teachers like to take credit for the successes of their students and blame their failures on parents and the students themselves. Parents and the public often reciprocate by blaming student failure on teachers. The truth is that whether we are talking about the specific proficiencies that students demonstrate or the attitudes and habits of mind they develop, myriad factors, too difficult to untangle, cooperate in the result.

Rebutting Alternative Formulations

Many may resist my approach and its conclusions. Some may challenge what they perceive to be its implicit political stance; others, its educational stance. Consider possible objections from the first group. Some readers may conclude that only those of us with a secular or scientific orientation could subscribe to the three aspirations, particularly to the injunction to heed evidence and argument. I don't agree. Consider members of a separatist, traditional subculture, a religious group like the Amish, perhaps, or the Orthodox Jews or a Native American tribe, people whose strongest commitment is to the preservation of a way of life inherited from their ancestors centuries ago.

Members of such a separatist group must surely recognize that they constitute a precarious island of tradition in the vast sea of a dynamic mainstream culture. In such circumstances, blindly and mechanically aping the patterns of conduct of their ancestors will only close the path to future sustainability. The members will have to continually decide what constitutes the indispensable core of their civilization and what is the expendable wrapping; which accommodations to the external culture will provide a space for them to develop their own traditions and which will subvert their core commitments. In order to meet such challenges, they will need to carefully consider evidence from the wider culture as well as from their own sacred teachings. So long as the context in which they live is dynamic, they will want to maintain a commitment to the three aspirations identified above, even though their own understanding of what constitutes relevant evidence or what kind of learning needs to be sustained throughout a lifetime may not always coincide with that of their more secular neighbors. Imagine children in such a community, exposed as they surely will be to the images, if not the realities, of alternative ways of life. Would not their parents want them to appreciate the *reasons* they should cleave to the traditional way of life rather than abandon it? I believe they would.

Some readers with left-leaning notions may have had their suspicions aroused by my use of the pronoun *we* throughout the original discussion of the key aspirations. To whom was I referring? These readers would point out that the pronoun masks the fact that our society is divided—some would say fatally divided—by gender and across class and racial lines. These divisions, it will be alleged, are reflected and perpetuated in the different kinds of schools and different programs within schools that enroll different segments of the population. It will be contended, therefore, that my use of *we* denies this reality and, hence, perpetuates it.

Nothing that I have said so far is intended to minimize these inequalities. It would take a knave or a fool to deny them, though people of goodwill may disagree about whether the educational system is the best place to remedy them. In any case the topic must and will be addressed in Chapter Seven. Nothing that I've said to this point requires that we all study the same subjects in the same way. But I ask those critics who object to my *we:* Which segment of the population would fail to endorse each of the three aspirations I identify? Is not the disposition and capacity to weigh the evidence precisely what makes possible your own trenchant analysis? Surely you wouldn't wish to deprive your descendants of the capacity to reach the same conclusions should the situation remain unchanged. Consider your present readers among the younger generation. Don't you want them to be impressed by the evidence and argument you muster in support of your position as well as by the sincerity and intensity of your convictions? I hope these are rhetorical questions.

Communitarians are likely to be disturbed by my framing the argument in terms of what individuals want for their own children. Isn't there too much emphasis on the individual and not enough on the community, they will say? Shouldn't our schools emphasize a commitment to strong, stable communities? My argument does not seek to undermine adherence to communities, even highly traditional communities. But we must recognize that the United States is not so much a single community as a collection of diverse communities. The aspirations we have for schooling, particularly for public schooling, must honor the commitments of people whose allegiances rest with very different kinds of communities. My conception tries to do this. It is not inimical to community but plays no favorites among communities.

I turn now to objections that focus on the educational stance. Readers will distrust my emphasis on the development of the *rational* faculties. It is just this perspective, they may believe, that is responsible for the troubles we are in, and for the mischief we, the allegedly advanced civilizations, have caused in other parts of the world. On what basis could they make such a claim? Surely, it must rest on evidence more solid than their own feelings or intuitions? Presumably, they would be prepared to offer such evidence. If that's so, then they ought to welcome my emphasis on students' developing a respect for evidence. Respect for evidence does not require that we worship "cold" rationality.

But why, I hear this objector continuing, do you privilege intellectual development over moral or emotional or physical development as the central purpose of schooling? What is the objector getting at? Possibly, to take a concrete example, that learning to care for the homeless is more important than being adept at quantitative reasoning. Now what, we may ask, might the objector mean by "learning to care for the homeless"? She might mean learning to put ourselves in their place. I agree. The capacity to learn includes the capacity to learn about both yourself and other people and schooling should enlarge that capacity.

But learning to care for the homeless might also mean learning to respond intelligently to the social problem of homelessness. Emptying our pockets when we are accosted by homeless people is now believed not to be an effective way to care for them. Why not? Because of *evidence* about the results of such instinctive caring. Unless we learn to respect that evidence, our good intentions may do more harm than good. Of course, the relevant evidence is based on inferences drawn from studies of selected homeless populations. Can such inferences be trusted? Here is where familiarity with quantitative reasoning is useful, indeed, indispensable. Our ability to respond intelligently to homelessness may ultimately depend on our capacity to understand quantitative reasoning as well as on our capacity for empathy.

An objector who does not quarrel with my focus on intellectual development may challenge the way I've formulated my three aspirations: "Since you're talking about the aspirations we have for our children's schooling rather than what we can expect schools to actually deliver, why not say that we hope our children will develop a deep understanding of the various fields of knowledge, or something of the kind? I can see that, too, is an ideal and even though it may be unlikely to be accomplished, it's at least more in line with what teachers and other educators think they're doing."

I deny that my aspirations are unrealistic except perhaps for the cognitively disabled. On the contrary, my aspirations are consonant with a democratic society's commitments to all its children. Suppose our goal were that all students develop an understanding of the various fields of knowledge, such as mathematics, including one year of calculus. What are the likely policies deriving from such a commitment? First, that we would seek to have as many students as possible achieve a mastery of calculus, and second, that we would need to develop indicators of such mastery that teachers could use as targets for their students.

What's wrong with these policies? For one thing, they would almost immediately lead to sorting the population into three groups: those likely to succeed without an intensive pedagogical effort, those whose success would depend on such an effort, and those who would be unlikely to succeed no matter how much effort was expended. Any prudent educator would avoid expending more than token resources on the the first and third groups. Also, an effort to get as many students as possible to pass the calculus exam runs the risk of subverting their interest in mathematics. A focus on recipes needed to solve test problems rather than on understanding underlying principles often extinguishes rather than kindles a disposition to continue learning mathematics—as many students of college calculus will attest. The key aspirations I've set, by contrast, while not ruling out any forms of ability grouping and tracking—something that will be discussed later—do not permit us either to trade off a disposition to learn for a specified level of mastery or to focus our concerns on one part of the population to the detriment of another. The reasoning behind our thought experiment bears this out: wanting the best for our great-grandchildren but not being sure of either their natural endowments or of the social circumstances they will be born into, we would take a grave risk by formulating aspirations that would sacrifice the prospects of any group of children.

What if our goal were that all students master some less ambitious inventory of knowledge or skills, that they develop some set of *minimal* competencies, say a mastery of mathematics through elementary algebra? Such a policy is reflected in statewide standards set by a number of states and may be the direction taken by the emerging national-standards movement. If the proportion of successful passes on national tests were to be tied to substantial rewards or penalties, instructional efforts would probably be concentrated on those who needed the most help to reach the cutoff. Here we run the risk of neglecting those who need only a little tutelage to pass the test, of weakening *their* disposition to sustain their learning. Recall again that the key aspirations I have identified must apply equally to all children.

A practical educator might reject my formulation because of the difficulty in evaluating students according to my criteria. We can tell whether a student knows how to find the area of a circle, but can we tell if a student has maintained a capacity or desire to learn? There is admittedly no easy way. Teachers derive clues from the kind of efforts students make, from their level of confidence in tackling new challenges, their degree of distractibility, their inclination to go beyond what is required, and so on.

My aspirations do not translate easily into tests that can be given or letter grades that can be awarded. That does not imply, however, that these aspirations require the abolition of a conventional grading system based on academic accomplishment. What it does imply is that any system of student evaluation selected for a specific context must itself be justified by the extent to which it is believed to promote the three key aspirations. In many cases, the requirements of student evaluation dictate the nature of the educational program and, hence, the aims actually served by that program. Often, the prime audience and beneficiaries of the evaluation system are not the students at all, but admissions officers of selective colleges or future employers.[5]

My mention of future employers will elicit another familiar objection: "Thus far, you've spoken of the educational aspirations we should have for children, but you've said nothing about the particular roles the schools are preparing them for. Don't we want the schools to graduate students who are capable of becoming productive workers in the economy of the twenty-first century? Don't we need students who are ready to become active, informed citizens?" There is currently much talk of the need for a "smarter" workforce, a workforce required to be more flexible, more adaptable to changing technological conditions. Suppose this is true. Just because the nature of the changes is unpredictable, it would be shortsighted to train students to work in the industries of the present. In a changing economy, where skills often become obsolete, a workforce that possesses the capacity and the desire to learn possesses everything an employer could ask for.

There is a danger in attempting to adapt the purposes of schooling to the labor needs of business and industry. Suppose that at some future time only a small proportion of the workforce is asked to solve difficult problems on the job. Suppose, as some argue, that this is actually the case now. If preparation for employment were our paramount concern, why wouldn't we focus our educational efforts on identifying and nurturing that fraction, neglecting the majority? I trust that you recoil at the suggestion. We all know that a changing world will require people whose disposition to learn has not been stifled, even if that disposition is not needed in the workplace. If the workplace of the future does not require the increased problem-solving capabilities that some are anticipating, leisure activities that permit people to develop their talents and capabilities will become all the more important. Of course, regardless of whether educators set their sights by the current or projected needs of the workplace, schools exist in an economic context that cannot simply be ignored. My discussion of inequalities in Chapter Seven explicitly takes the economy into account.

The dependence of democracy on education is often asserted. To be sure, democratic government requires active, informed citizens, but the disposition to follow the evidence and to keep on learning is not valuable because it makes democracy possible. Rather, it is the other way around. Democracy is the form of organizing our collective life that makes it least likely that evidence bearing on what we ought collectively to do will be suppressed or ignored. A monarchy or dictatorship that permits no legitimate opposition is unlikely to jeopardize its stability by seeking or publicizing evidence that casts doubt on its decisions. Parties or factions in a democracy, however, must attempt to build a majority through persuasion. In the course of attempting to persuade the electorate, incumbents will try to trumpet their successes, while those trying to unseat them will challenge the incumbents' assessment of the record. In the course of debates and campaigns, evidence favoring the competing parties and candidates and evidence damaging to them will necessarily have a role in the contest for votes.

Democratic government is valuable, however, not only because a decision reached after due deliberation by interested parties is more likely to be in the interests of the majority rather than the minority; it is also valuable because, at its best, it guarantees each citizen a voice and provides us all an opportunity to enrich our understanding and develop our powers. This opportunity for development derives partly from the activist role a citizen may assume in a democracy like ours but, more importantly, from exposure to points of view and ideas very different from our own.

Finally, educational conservatives are likely to be troubled by my line of argument. Let me address them directly: you think that the essential task of education lies, not in the cultivation of dispositions, but in the initiation of a new generation into appreciation of the works in the arts and sciences that are the pinnacles of our civilization's achievements. Fine, so far as it goes, but in what does that appreciation consist? Regurgitating information about great books for teachers but never opening them at home after graduation? Successfully answering questions in class about the scientific method but denying evidence that flies in the face of a favorite conviction? Being able to recount the causes of World War I in a coherent essay but not being able to recognize that the present situation in Europe is not totally unprecedented? Surely you do not intend people to spend about fifteen thousand hours of their young lives in classrooms only to exit with such a shallow appreciation of their heritage? It is only by placing my key dispositions at the top of your agenda that you educational conservatives can hope to initiate the next generation into a tradition that will be vital and compelling throughout their lives.

Perhaps a final thought experiment will help the educational conservative to appreciate if not adopt my point of view. Think of a child you care about and think of some school subject to which you are entirely indifferent—Latin, perhaps, or trigonometry, or English grammar, or earth science. Imagine that this child's school's curriculum is concentrated on that particular subject to the age of seventeen to the virtual exclusion of all else; imagine that at the end of her schooling, though she has learned little about most subjects, she has developed a genuine concern for examining the evidence on any issue and retains a keen desire to learn new subjects in and out of school. Now imagine a second hypothetical state of affairs in which this same child has accumulated perfect scores on achievement tests in a half-dozen different school subjects. In the process, however, she has lost the desire to continue learning without extrinsic motivation and she manifests little effort to seek or consider evidence regarding any of the questions and problems she confronts.

Which hypothetical situation would you prefer? If your primary concern were social status, you might prefer the second situation because your child's entry to college and subsequent social standing would be more secure. To the extent that you saw your role as that of an educator, you would, according to my view, have to prefer the first scenario. For all its short-term deficiencies, the child's education here is *vital*, while in the second hypothetical situation it is inert, available only to impress examiners, like a formal dress that permits entry to an exclusive dance but does nothing to transform the character of its wearer.

Fortunately, the educational choices we have to make are never this stark; a single school subject would probably be no more nutritious than food from a single food group. The artificiality of the two situations results from the fact that successful mastery of school subjects and the disposition to learn are normally but not always mutually reinforcing. Our experience as parents and teachers tells us that they are sometimes in tension, which is why it is important for educators and for those who care about schooling, which is to say almost all of us, to be clear about what schools should do for children.

One last question before concluding this chapter: Why do I place so much value on being disposed to care about evidence and to keep on learning? Are these dispositions intrinsically good or are they only instrumentally valuable for the pursuit of a satisfying life? In a static world, it is possible that such dispositions would not be of much use, but in our unstable world there is little doubt that these dispositions have instrumental value. Without them, we could not learn from our mistakes, and in an unpredictable world, it is almost certain that we shall make mistakes. Even in a stable world, such dispositions would be of use in solidifying and defending our own convictions. Suppose that we believe that the nuclear family is too valuable a human invention to jeopardize. Will that conviction be persuasive to others or ultimately to us if it rests only on the fact that our parents or the Bible said so? Wouldn't and shouldn't evidence from our own experience and that of systematic students of the family favoring that hypothesis strengthen our own convictions? Suppose, however, that no such evidence can be found. Wouldn't it be somewhat foolish to continue maintaining the belief?

Far from being hostile to the Western tradition, let me acknowledge in closing that at the bottom of my conception of education is an article of faith that has been central to that tradition for at least two millenia—the conviction that human beings have distinctive powers of understanding, practical mastery, and aesthetic expressiveness, and that the development of these powers brings deep and lasting satisfaction.

Chapter Three

Curriculum

In the previous chapter, I made two explicit assumptions that should not go unquestioned in a work that is focused on examining fundamental educational questions. I assumed that schools should continue to exist and that their primary focus was to be their students' intellectual development. Let's consider each of these in turn.

Why Schools?

It is generally accepted by U.S. citizens that schooling will occupy a substantial proportion of all children's time between the ages of about six till about eighteen, and that the school's primary but by no means exclusive responsibility is the inculcation of the basic tools of literacy and numeracy along with some intellectual grasp of the world the children live in. These understandings are widely and deeply shared; it would take very compelling reasons to dislodge them. And yet, it must be recognized that the idea of compulsory schooling through secondary school is relatively new in human history. The reality of mass compulsory schooling from kindergarten through high school is not even a hundred years old in this country.

We should not forget, moreover, that there are still human communities that flourish, or at least sustain themselves, without formal schooling. Pockets of resistance to compulsory schooling exist even in our own country; indeed, there is growing participation and interest in home schooling in every state. It would be hard to contend that no child can hope to lead a happy and successful adult life without going to school, and some might even be prepared to argue that for many children schools do as much harm as good, even in the area of intellectual development.

The rationale for setting up schools and compelling attendance in them is familiar but needs to be restated here. The dispositions and capabilities adults wish to impart to the next generation are too complex to be acquired either haphazardly, by participation in and observation of adult activities, or by formal apprenticeships. Although this proposition is scarcely deniable, we take it largely on faith that the intellectual development we seek to foster takes about twelve years to nurture and needs to be conducted in institutions designed for that purpose by people specifically trained for that pursuit. I say "on faith" because it is difficult to test out such convictions, and because exceptions found among graduates of home schools or alternative schools in which lessons are optional suggest that the *necessity* of twelve years of schooling might well be questioned, the more so in an age of videodiscs and home computers.

Even if it were granted that a long period of tutelage is required to nurture the desired capacities and dispositions, that would still not necessarily lead to mandating attendance at a *school*. We could imagine an educational system composed of a large army of private tutors who were available for hire by individual parents. Tutorial arrangements were familiar to many of our ancestors, especially to our European ancestors in the previous two centuries, but tutorial arrangements flourished before it was expected that *all* children would require a formal education. I think it must be conceded that the number of children is simply too great and the number of potential tutors too limited to make this a live option for us here and now. If we were asked to redesign our society from scratch, assuming that such a task would even be intelligible, we might come up with quite different educational arrangements, but we have to begin with the fact that, for us, schools appear to be an almost self-evident way to provide for the intellectual development of our progeny.

Most people in the United States take for granted the existence not just of schools, but of schools supported by taxpayers, run by local government, and attended by the vast majority of the population. Widespread acceptance of government-run schools reflects more than simply a reluctant concession to the scarcity and high price of private tutors; whether that commitment to public schools can be defended on philosophical grounds will be the subject of Chapter Six. The attachment to public schooling felt even by many of those whose own children attend private school does suggest, however, that the institution has a deeper hold on our loyalties than would be expected if it were simply a cheaper or more efficient substitute for private tutors. This ideal is, I think, brought out by the original name of the institution, the "common" school.

The name *common school* conjures up a nineteenth-century image of children from all parts of town and the surrounding countryside congregating in the same building to learn their lessons in the three R's and in citizenship. That image connects to images we have of ourselves as a people with a long and continuing tradition of settlement, migration, and immigration, fleeing religious persecution and economic deprivation, antagonistic not only to aristocracy but to class divisions and separatist sects. Many who have studied our history and the realities of public schooling have, as we know, found this image to be largely mythological, playing a role in our political life somewhere between that of harmless fantasy and cruel deception.

I do not wish to enter the debate concerning the extent of the discrepancy between the myth and the reality.[1] That such a discrepancy exists, there is no doubt, but awareness of the gulf does not necessarily destroy the power of the myth, though it may weaken it. My point is that the loyalties evoked by the idea of public schools have always been connected to ideals and aspirations that went beyond their agreed-upon primary purpose, intellectual development.

Today some reformers propose that schools once again enlarge their mission, while others, decrying the burdens already piled on the institution, seek to prune the school of its ancillary responsibilities. Whatever the resolution of this tension, nothing has altered the fact that academic learning, though not always the central concern of children, is still perceived by the adult population that sustains schools to be at the core of what formal education is all about. Despite the oft-cited anti-intellectual propensities of Americans, the elimination of driver's education and even of football from public schools is thinkable—in some communities fiscal crisis has actually led to cancellation of the football season—while the elimination of mathematics is unthinkable.

I grant that whatever loyalties we may feel toward our own school are often more likely to be connected to Friday night football games than to algebra class. But we all realize that not everyone needs to learn to play football and that school is not the only place young people can play or learn to play the game. We do think all children need to learn to read and write and understand the world. Although many of us have legitimate reservations about existing schools and some of us would prefer to teach our children at home, I think it's fair to say that if schools somehow disappeared for a generation, our children would be very likely to reinvent them.

Which Knowledge Should Be Taught?

We have already seen that what we want schools to do for children is best formulated in terms of rather general capacities and dispositions, but we also made it clear that there is no such thing as generic learning around which the school's program of studies might be organized. The traditional subjects, such as history, mathematics, and the arts, provide the most obvious but not the only framework for thinking about what specifically school should try to teach. This traditional approach to curriculum selection would lead us to include items like the following:

- Proving a theorem in geometry
- Placing a historical event in context or interpreting a historical document
- Learning how to scan a poem, discover a novelist's point of view, or look at a painting

- Measuring atmospheric air pressure or demonstrating the conservation of momentum
- Understanding Avogadro's number, the history of race relations in the United States, or harmony in music.

The organization of school subjects based on the academic disciplines has existed as long as there have been schools, but given present dissatisfaction with schools and given the fact that some of the alternatives to the traditional curriculum have had vigorous proponents, especially among progressive educators, the question of what to teach is far from closed. The conventional organization, say its critics, suffers from two handicaps. Although most children are naturally curious, it will take several years of schooling before they learn to fit their questions into the categories presented by the traditional school subjects. In learning to make distinctions that must appear artificial to them at the outset, children too often learn the art of pleasing teachers rather than satisfying their own curiosity. That is one reason why progressive educators bent on adapting educational institutions to the "nature" of children have always found the conventional subject matter divisions arbitrary and unnatural.

By the time schools teach them to divide problems into algebra problems, history problems, and so on, students are able to recognize that few of the actual problems confronting people fall under just one rubric. This adds to the sense many students develop that school questions are cut off from the world of living problems. It is not that the traditional organization fails to deal with students' personal problems. Few would expect schools to do that. Rather, the concern is that even the problems we face as a collectivity, problems whose solution clearly requires understanding and wisdom, can't be forced into the pigeonholes provided by the academic disciplines. Think, for example, of an issue that is on our national agenda at the time of this writing, the best way to respond to the widespread use of illegal drugs. Thinking through such a problem depends on reasonable acquaintance with a substantial number of different subjects: chemistry, medicine, economics, politics, ethics, statistics, history, and sociology, to name the most obvious. If the conventional framework for thinking about the curriculum has its limitations, can we envision alternatives? Indeed, we can. We might, for example, organize the curriculum around things children will have to know when they are adults. Here are some items that might be found on such a list:

- Safe driving
- Planning a budget for a family
- Planning nutrition for healthy eating
- Figuring out your taxes
- Finding a suitable job
- Learning how to communicate with your spouse
- Dressing for success
- Taking care of babies
- Understanding the nature and operation of labor unions
- Understanding the social security system

It is ironic that progressives—proponents of the "life-adjustment" education fashionable in the 1940s—who presumably understood that thinking about teaching must begin with children, not subjects, should have devised curricula focused on practical life tasks that *adults* need to perform. Progressive educators may be right in thinking that teachers need to take advantage of what students care about, but how many young people care about home mortgages or infant nutrition? Whatever is learned about such matters is likely to be either forgotten or obsolete by the time the problem actually presents itself five or ten years later. School classrooms, it must be added, are usually not well designed or equipped for such learning. Besides, if the school has cultivated an ability and a propensity to learn, it will not be difficult for students to find out what they need to know about such matters once the need arises.

We might imagine the curriculum designed explicitly around

the interests that children bring with them to school. Of course, some children have interests that lead quite naturally into the conventional academic subjects—"Why is the sky blue?" "Why doesn't Billy's mom live with him?" Most young people's interests, however, run in different directions. A curriculum designed around those interests would include items like these:

- Improving Nintendo strategies
- Learning how to flirt
- Drawing superheroes
- Playing better poker
- Pumping iron
- "Souping up" cars
- Learning how to resist peer pressure while remaining popular
- Learning how movies are made
- Understanding the National Basketball Association draft
- Understanding the popular music business

We might think of using such topics as a way of appealing to young people and as a starting point for a journey that will ultimately go in other directions. This may make educational sense: if some children who come to school with short attention spans and few intellectual resources can become engaged long enough to develop habits of mind that will serve them well later, such topics may have educational value. If children's curiosity is tapped, we may be able to kindle the desire to learn that we are ultimately hoping to nurture. In fact, given the key aspirations we have for children, we will not view the items on this list with total contempt; for some children and some situations, these items will provide a gateway to the development of those dispositions we are ultimately concerned with.

Leaving aside the fact that no adult community would sustain a school whose curriculum was limited to such topics, an entire school diet made up of them would not ultimately prove nutritious.

These topics lack the potential for sustained development. The resulting learning would be no more than a collection of unrelated fragments, generated by interest that is quickly kindled and just as quickly extinguished. Rather than helping children redirect their attention to subjects that will truly develop their capacity to learn, these topics essentially limit them to just those things that are familiar to them, most often because of the impact of successful marketing campaigns. Deep down, even the average seven-year-old senses that Nintendo is really a diversion from the more serious things in life, not an engagement with them.

In difficult times like these—are there ever easy ones?—people often accuse the next generation of failing to adhere to traditional norms of ethical conduct. Typically the schools will be blamed for their inattention to the inculcation of morality and there will be calls, both mellow and strident, to place moral learning at the center of schooling. A curriculum that took those calls seriously would focus on items like these:

- Learning how to criticize someone without destroying a relationship
- Knowing when to tell the honest truth and when to shade it a bit
- Getting help when you need it
- Learning how to keep going when you feel like quitting
- Understanding the difference between what a person has done and what he or she is responsible for doing
- Understanding the differences, if any, between men and women and what responses those differences demand

There is a sense in which all of life contributes to learning the items found here. It is clear that, whether deliberately or not, teachers and schools affect students' development in this domain. It would be impossible for them not to. Does the teacher accept a hastily scrawled assignment or insist that the student redo it? Does he accept the student's word for her inability to do her homework or demand confirmation from home? Does he call on girls less often than boys in math class? Does the school treat all those who violate its rules the same way or are some more equal than others? Every action taken or not taken, every routine and procedure, even the school architecture, sends signals to children, signals that affect the way they view themselves, their peers, their society, and their rights and responsibilities.

That said, however, it seems to me that moral education ought not to take center stage, nor can it provide the basis for organizing the program of studies, at least not in the public schools. There are two reasons for this. First of all, despite the considerable moral consensus that exists in our communities—does anyone really support the defacing of public property or the exploitation of the weak students by the strong?—efforts to formulate and teach a uniform moral code that would enlist everyone's support would only highlight the areas where adults disagree and disagree passionately. To what extent should young people be required to obey their elders unquestioningly? To what extent do homosexuals deserve the protection and support of the community? At what age is it appropriate for young people to begin drinking? to make their own friends? to begin sexual relationships? Does wearing tight clothes constitute an invitation to verbal sexual harassment? Trying to generate enough public consensus on such explosive issues to design a moral education curriculum for *all* students is a hopeless task.

Second, the school's potential as moral educator is severely limited by its structure. Recall that for the most part schools contain hundreds or even thousands of students, organized into classes of about twenty-five to thirty-five students with one teacher. The students may be with the same teacher for as much as six hours each weekday in early elementary school, but in middle and high schools for as little as forty-five minutes a day, five times a week. Under such conditions, it is rare for a teacher and student to know each other well or to form strong bonds. Indeed, since no adult can be expected to form strong bonds with so many young people under such conditions, the demands of fairness discourage the formation of such bonds with only a few. Although some young people will always try to model themselves after favorite teachers, the majority of students will not look to their teachers for either affection or personal guidance. Without a chance for teacher and students to get to know each other well in a variety of situations, the potential for the schoolteacher to play a central role in the psychic life of individual students is diminished. Only an adult whose "I'm proud of you" or "You really let me down" means something important to a child can be a potent moral educator.

It may be that some students have no adults who care specially about them; under those circumstances the teacher may be the only adult who interacts regularly with them and has a stake in their welfare, but the setting is far from ideal from the point of view of moral education. Rather than saddling teachers with the responsibility of acting as parent substitutes in cases where parents are unavailable, we need to be generous and imaginative in creating alternatives. Big brothers and sisters recruited from among college students, surrogate grandparents recruited from the ranks of the retired, counselors at summer camps, after-school coaches of chess or basketball—these people provide the kinds of relationships that need to be built upon and invested in.

Of course, the study of history and literature always presents opportunities for moral education, opportunities that deserve to be exploited. Before mass media, noble deeds of legendary heroes recounted in books or orally may have been potent influences, but it is doubtful that schoolbooks could counteract the immediacy and drawing power of movies and television shows. While the personal struggles and moral quandaries of fictional or historical characters can stimulate thoughtful consideration of issues in English or social studies classes, there is generally something inauthentic about such discussions. Students are quick to detect and provide the kinds of responses teachers expect or approve of. A curriculum organized around central questions of how to live and what kind of person to be is more likely to teach hypocrisy than any moral virtue.

A final way of thinking about the curriculum derives from one of the criticisms made of the conventional framework—that authentic problems always exceed the reach of a single academic discipline. The curriculum might, itself, be organized around more authentic tasks. Items on such a list would take the following form:[2]

- Designing a policy to deal with the narcotics problem
- Knowing how to lobby for legislation
- Confronting the problem of world hunger and malnutrition
- Designing an experiment for the space shuttle
- Publishing a newspaper about the Civil War
- Producing a television show about adolescents
- Mounting a Renaissance fair or arts festival
- Designing, building, and programming a robot

Many progressive educators have and would favor such a way of thinking about the curriculum. Problems that are the exclusive prerogative of a single discipline are pretty much limited to professionals in those disciplines. Because authentic problems are more likely to be unresolved, in contrast to textbook problems whose solution is known, what evidence bears on them and what conclusions ought to be drawn from that evidence are likely to be real issues. This makes them ideal for developing the key dispositions and capacities identified in the last chapter.

Some items on the above list reflect challenges we have to meet collectively rather than individually, so these topics are adapted to school settings in a couple of ways. Discussing such questions in a group of thirty is a good way to develop an understanding of diverse points of view as well as a sense of whether an issue is important or trivial, difficult or easy to resolve. Moreover, the learning needed to master many of the challenges straddles several disciplines, so there is an opportunity for smaller groups to work together on aspects of the larger question and then to share their contributions with the other students. Since the ability to work in groups is often prized outside school, this mode of organization fosters dispositions that will be very useful later on.

Let us consider some reasons *not* to organize the curriculum around authentic problems. One is that the problems that have the biggest hold on us today might turn out to look quite different in five or ten years. Ways to deal with narcotics might no longer be a live issue when today's students graduate from school. Even if this were so, however, since our ultimate aspiration is the development of dispositions and capacities, this limitation does not loom large.

A more serious obstacle is posed by the fact that understanding and confronting the problems identified under this rubric are impossible without considerable disciplinary knowledge. For example, grasping the dimensions of the drug problem and evaluating possible responses will be impossible without some expertise in economics and quantitative reasoning. We could introduce disciplinary expertise as it is needed to work on particular issues. This would be advantageous because the need for introducing certain ideas about the operation of markets or elementary statistics would have a clear motivation. On the other hand, students might fail to appreciate the richness and diversity of the disciplines themselves, just as when someone learns a foreign language by memorizing travel phrases from a Berlitz book.

Solutions to contemporary problems are dependent in a more profound sense on what we learn in the traditional disciplines. Our responses to narcotic substances are informed by core beliefs concerning individual responsibility and the role of government, the role of pleasure in life, and the distinction between "legitimate" and "illegitimate" pleasures. To be able to grasp these core ideas with some degree of objectivity rather than be prisoners of them requires an understanding of history and philosophy that is hard to convey in a merely ad hoc way.

Moreover, pressing the case for the traditional organization, such a system represents the way our civilization has until now organized what is known in order to revise, refine, and add to it, and, most important from our point of view, to *transmit* it. Progress in solving practical problems, such as the problem of drug addiction, often derives from advances in fields far removed from them, sometimes as the result of scientific or mathematical discoveries that were motivated by no practical concern at all. Whatever anti-intellectual currents flow through society, we recognize and honor the successful pursuit of knowledge and artistic expression for its own sake. Suppose that we organized the curriculum exclusively around authentic problems. How would we identify and educate those who are destined to push back the frontiers of science and the arts? Would we need a separate track for future artists and scientists?

Vigorously championed for over fifty years by some progressive educators, efforts to sustain an entire school curriculum organized around authentic problems have been notably unsuccessful. Of course, noteworthy projects do exist here and there: Seymour Papert's Lego-Logo workshop, in which elementary school students can build and program robots, trucks, and the like; the "microeconomy school," in which students simulate a small productive economy; and the Future Problem Solving Program, an extracurricular program in which students work in teams of four to design solutions to real problems.[3] Such programs, unfortunately, remain marginal in most schools and school systems. Why?

It must be recognized that in all but a tiny minority of cases, the school is organized almost exclusively around the traditional academic subjects. This means that teachers are trained to see themselves as imparters of particular academic disciplines or, in the case of elementary teachers, of most if not all the traditional subjects. Even teachers who may view their primary role as helping students to make sense of their lives or to feel good about themselves recognize that they are being paid to teach social studies or arithmetic or music—or all three in the case of elementary school teachers. A curriculum organized around authentic problems would require, in addition to teachers with strengths in more than one subject and a different view of what they were trying to accomplish, a more flexible organization of space and time. Increased flexibility requires a relaxation of bureaucratic procedures and cooperative planning by teachers from different departments, which are both very difficult to accomplish, especially in large, impersonal organizations dealing with potentially unruly students.

Such reorganization and retraining of personnel is not unthinkable, as successful examples show, but a dramatic change of orientation is not likely in the foreseeable future. I, myself, would encourage such efforts where they exist or are proposed, if only to find out what they can accomplish. There is little doubt in my mind that the defects the progressives identified in the traditional organization of subject matter are real. The learning diet is much too one-sided, and I have no doubt that periodic supplements of authentic projects that resist disciplinary pigeonholing would be salutary. Papert's vision of students involved in projects of their own choosing, projects whose completion requires mastery of traditional subject matter, is an appealing one. The question, from my point of view, is whether a steady diet of such projects would be more likely to enhance students' respect for evidence and their desire and capacity to learn than the traditional fare. It is cause for regret that answers to this question are left to speculation. Sadly, the evident failure of many students to thrive on traditional educational fare has not led to experiments with alternative educational diets over long enough periods of time to see whether they could overcome educational malnutrition. Such experiments deserve our strong support.

At the same time, Dewey's intellectual descendants cannot turn away from unpleasant facts: progressive exhortations for dramatic changes in the way we think about the school curriculum over more than fifty years have produced only a small coterie of converts among working teachers and principals. Without their commitment, the exhortations remain only so much verbiage.

Where, then, does this examination leave us? What adults will need to know is a misguided basis for organizing the curriculum; what children want to know has a very limited, but not to be despised, place in our educational scheme, especially in the earliest years. Moral knowledge should never be ignored, since moral messages are communicated in any case, yet it should not be the primary focus of schools, especially not of public schools. Both authentic challenges and the traditional disciplines have strengths and limitations from the point of view of our key aspirations for children; neither deserves our exclusive allegiance. We should press for the inclusion of some authentic projects into the life of the school, but we neither want nor expect them to supplant the traditional mode of organizing knowledge for teaching.

School Subjects

Although there is every reason to expect that, for the most part, the curriculum will continue to be organized around the familiar academic subjects, there still remains the question of what this means and implies. Let's begin by reminding ourselves that these subjects are not stable bodies of knowledge, but that they are continually evolving. The expansion in the sheer quantity of what is known has resulted, in part, from a vast increase in specialization. A few hundred years ago, it was possible for learned men (women were, by and large, excluded) to grasp most of what there was to know. About a hundred years ago, when John Dewey was appointed professor at the University of Chicago, the fields of psychology and philosophy were still combined in a single department. Today, at larger universities, not only are each of these departments separate, but there are typically two separate psychology departments that overlap only marginally. Specialization sometimes gives rise to reactions in the other direction, and new subjects such as cognitive science have been created, through the merger of branches of older fields of study. Still other branches of study, like computer science, emerge from the invention of new technologies.

Of course, while much more is known, our increased understanding also gives us an appreciation of how much there is that we don't know. The effort to understand and effectively confront the scourge of acquired immunodeficiency syndrome (AIDS) provides a ready illustration. While enormous progress has been made in a decade of concentrated effort to understand the myriad dimensions of the disease, no cure or vaccine is even in sight.

The common image of a knowledge "explosion" is, perhaps, more apt than its users intend, however, for there is not only the already-mentioned expansion of scholarly information that is reflected in the thousands of scholarly journals now being published on a regular basis, but there is also a great deal of debate and dissension, sometimes exceedingly acrimonious, within an established discipline about the nature, accomplishments, and prospects of that discipline. Such contentiousness is found in fields ranging from music and the arts to literary studies, the social sciences, and even some of the natural sciences. The very ideas that made possible the growth in our knowledge have been employed to undermine our confidence in the reliability and value of that knowledge. The growth of knowledge is seen sometimes as central, sometimes as irrelevant, and sometimes as damaging to our hopes of creating better lives on the planet.

How should we think of the different fields of study from the educational point of view? Perhaps the most suggestive image comes from what at first blush might appear an unlikely source, conservative philosopher Michael Oakeshott.[4] Oakeshott likened the major fields of study to human languages that take time and effort to acquire. What he meant to highlight was that learning a subject, like learning a language, ought to consist of acquiring a means of understanding and expression rather than a particular body of doctrine or information. Each field, like each language, has its distinctive vocabulary and syntax that must be mastered in order to participate in conversations with those who have learned to "speak" it, but neither the syntax nor the vocabulary is static, and neither limits what might be said.

Oakeshott took mathematics, the natural sciences, the humanities (which for him include the arts), and the social sciences to be the primary "language" families, and despite the controversies I have mentioned, these basic divisions do correspond to recognizable differences in outlook and approach. From the point of view of Oakeshott's metaphor, what appears to me to be most striking and regrettable is that the various subjects are presented to students, not as languages at all, but precisely as bodies of information and doctrine. From the students' point of view, the main difference between, say, biology and history is that the former comprises information about organisms and their parts; the latter, information about historical epochs and their parts. The main exceptions to this are music and the fine arts, which occupy a marginal and often vulnerable place in the curriculum.

It is not entirely unexpected that the various subjects should be presented as so many bodies of information. First, mastery of vocabulary *is* part of learning any language; until an initial stock of words is available for use a novice will neither understand nor be able to communicate. Second, the structure of classrooms as well as the expectations of students and parents make departure from the vision of schooling as the imparting of information problematic. There is little doubt in my mind, however, that although the primary concepts and modes of reasoning may need to be introduced rather directly, the distinctive "syntax" of each different field of study cannot be effectively conveyed in this way. Moreover, from the point of view of our key aspiration that students should care about the evidence bearing on conclusions, the presentation of a subject matter as a large collection of bits of knowledge is singularly unfortunate. The kind and quality of evidence needed to make judgments within a domain and assessment of the quality of that evidence are probably best learned in connection with questions where no single correct answer is agreed on by all experts.

Some readers will think that the doubtful or contested propositions found on the frontiers of the various fields of learning require years of study to even understand, much less grapple with. I think this belief is exaggerated. There are many hotly debated issues, the cause of dinosaur extinction and the origin of gender differences, to name two, that students can grapple with even while they lack the expertise and sophistication of the scholars debating them. When this is impossible, voyages to established conclusions in a field may be traveled again by novices in order to yield a sense of adventure and mastery.

Gifted teachers have always found ways of making it possible for novices to *do*, not just learn about, poetry, archaeology, history, biology, or mathematics. Of course, novices' "conclusions" and "discoveries" are not likely to be valuable contributions from the expert's point of view, but that is irrelevant. Many visitors to classrooms who see nothing unusual when very young students paint, work in clay, or compose poems and stories would expect students to *do* history, science, mathematics, or philosophy only in graduate school.

This need not be so. In the language of my metaphor, students early on ought to sense the excitement of beginning to use a "language" they are in the process of learning rather than having to memorize thousands of vocabulary words before actually communicating. What might this mean for the kinds of activities children would actually engage in? Let me illustrate with one subject, history. Students might be given facsimiles of a number of documents relating to some important event, such as the outbreak of a war or a key election. The students might then be asked to reconstruct a historical narrative accounting for that event. The various accounts could be compared and evaluated. Questions about the objectivity of history might even be discussed with sophisticated students.

I have noted that contentious debate is rife in all fields; though sometimes distressing, it contributes to the vitality of many academic subjects on university campuses. The vitality resulting from vigorous intellectual disagreement does not, unfortunately, find its way into the textbooks that purvey school subjects to learners in schools. Textbook publishers reflect these debates and uncertainties only by adding or deleting information in order to respond to different constituencies while hoping to offend none. The texts remain, for the most part, repositories of information that appear to represent no particular point of view, written in prose lacking any distinctive authorial voice.

Doesn't all this contentiousness make it difficult to achieve consensus about what to teach? Indeed, it does. But should we even *seek* consensus on what to teach? Recall that in my view, schooling should aim to foster rather general dispositions and capacities. Given that aspiration, there is no reason to think that all children need to learn the same things; indeed, there is good reason to think that the enormous diversity in students' cultural and social backgrounds would make it most unlikely that these key aspirations could be promoted by means of a uniform curriculum for all. Let me offer a nutritional analogy. Suppose we have as our aim that everyone should enjoy a nutritious and healthy diet. Should we prescribe the very same meals or even the same foods for everyone? There is no reason to. Tastes and tolerances for foods differ; there is every reason to honor them.

Consensus about what specifically to teach is not nearly as important as many educational conservatives think. As has been noted many times, too much is known for any person to know much. If a thousand educators were asked to list the ten works that all students should have read by the time they finish high school, I doubt that we would find much agreement beyond possibly the U.S. Constitution. Of course, some common references facilitate communication, but they are amply provided for by the mass media. Perhaps we would be a better nation if everyone read the same books, but I see no reason to think so. Surely, it will be said, there are facts that everyone should know, such as the name of the present secretary of state. I agree, but since that gentleman took office only a year ago, the vast majority of the U.S. population *couldn't* have learned his name in school. The reason people are (or should be) shocked by the reported ignorance of so much of our population, assuming it to be true, is not that millions of people haven't learned anything in school, but that they appear not to *care* about national or world affairs. Surely, even E. D. Hirsch, Jr., would have to agree that committing his dictionary of cultural literacy to memory would do nothing to rectify that problem.

I can imagine a conservative educator saying, "Granted that there are no mandatory facts everyone should know, but surely there are masterpieces that are virtually mandatory. Isn't school *the* place where students may be expected to be exposed to Shakespeare's *Hamlet*, to Handel's *Messiah*, to Leonardo's *Mona Lisa?* Haven't these works met critical acclaim for centuries? Are we now to ignore them?" In responding, let us recall the nutritional analogy, used in this context by Dewey himself. Imagine that these works correspond to the finest gourmet meal available at the most elegant restaurant. Would such a meal be capable of being appreciated by all children at any time in their development? Could we not imagine children leaving such an occasion and vowing never to set foot in such an establishment again?

I do not deny that some masterpieces have provided pleasure and illumination in every age. These masterpieces should not be abandoned by the present generation, but consider: Does the force-feeding of great masterpieces to students in high school and college with insufficient life experience to appreciate them really engender the passionate attachment to "the best" that educational conservatives are seeking? We do want to strengthen students' capacity to make discerning judgments and to respect quality in the aesthetic as well as the scientific fields, and we won't be able to do that unless we expose them to works of quality, perhaps comparing these works to the more formulaic and crass ones they are acquainted with from prime-time television. But there is no *particular* work or set of works that is mandatory for people to appreciate or enjoy. From the point of view of developing their aesthetic sensibilities, which is more important: that students care about the quality of the television shows they watch, or that they be able to identify by artist and style the famous paintings hanging in the Louvre? Teachers and professors may think that in attending to the latter, they are attending to the former, but a day or evening in front of the tube will surely convince them otherwise. To reiterate, the conservative is not wrong in wishing that all adults could appreciate great works like *Hamlet* but in thinking that mandating its study by all high school seniors is a way of ensuring that appreciation.

Perhaps it would be useful to review the argument of this chapter. After reminding ourselves of the reasons schools exist, we focused on a variety of ways of thinking about the curriculum. The conventional framework provided by the academic disciplines does have drawbacks, but there are good reasons to think it will remain the primary, though I hope not the *exclusive*, basis for deciding about what knowledge schools should transmit. Schools need to teach the disciplines as living "languages" rather than as collections of facts. Finally, forging a consensus about what specifically to teach all children is neither necessary nor desirable.

Chapter Four

Teaching

Depending on how we look at it, teaching might be thought of either as an activity that is virtually effortless or as one of the most difficult tasks imaginable. There is a sense in which most of us who are not professional teachers do some deliberate teaching every day. As parents, we teach our children all kinds of things, such as how to tell time, how to ask for a cookie, or how to tell the serious from the playful. Even those of us who are not parents or grandparents do a surprising amount of teaching as well. Rare is the day when we are not called upon to give directions to a lost motorist, demonstrate a procedure to a new employee, report on our progress to a supervisor, or explain our behavior or position on an issue to a friend. Teaching, in the broadest sense of sharing what we know with others, is part of living. Our species survived for thousands of years before there were schools. Surely, we must be naturally equipped to be tolerably good teachers (and learners) or human communities would never have survived. Teaching is a natural activity. Or is it?

Mediocre and Exemplary Teachers

Imagine that you have just received a phone call from the principal of the public school a few blocks away: One of the first grade teachers has just called in sick; could you come over tomorrow morning and take over the class? Or, to fill in for a high school English teacher who is not feeling well, you are being asked to teach five classes of sophomore English, two classes in the college preparatory track, and three in the vocational track. (I am deliberately choosing subjects that appear to be within the competence of most readers of these pages.) I daresay that either prospect is enough to induce fear and trembling in most readers, perhaps even in those who have been teachers. Why should that be? What is there to be afraid of? My guess is that two concerns undermine your confidence: Can you elicit enough respect to prevent the students from running amok? and Do you know how to convey what you know in a way that they would find interesting, a way that would really help them become more competent readers and writers?

These questions reveal two respects in which school teaching is far from the effortless activity described above: first, most teaching is directed at groups of children whose interest in the subject, far from being a given, must be cultivated, and, second, knowing something doesn't mean that you know how to teach it effectively.

There is a sense in which the pervasiveness and effortlessness of informal teaching contributes both to our underestimating the difficulty of classroom teaching and to our being willing to tolerate mediocre teachers. The "natural" approach to teaching is to stand or sit in front of the group of students, to tell them what we know about the subject they are supposed to learn, to answer any questions they may have about our lesson, and to ask occasional questions to see whether they remember what we have just said. This approach is not obviously inadequate and, indeed, it is what you will find in most classrooms around the world.

Noelle Oxenhandler reminisces about such teaching at a Parisian lycée she attended a quarter of a century ago (I choose the example partly because French secondary education has often been an object of envy in this country):[1]

We sat for hours, mute as stones, in drafty, high-ceilinged rooms. The teachers spoke endlessly, and as they spoke we wrote down what they said word for word on graph paper in small plaid notebooks. . . . Every now and again, when a teacher felt she'd made an

important point, she'd say, "Underline and make a box around it."
The only times we spoke were fraught with terror.

"Lamontier!" a teacher might call out. "Stand up! Button your
smock! To the blackboard!"

"Yes, Madame."

"The Jura Mountains are composed of what kind of rock?"

"Boulders, Madame."

"*What?*"

"*Large* boulders, Madame."

Consider, now, an exemplary high school physics lesson
described by John T. Bruer in a recent article in a popular magazine
for teachers.[2] There are, of course, many ways of being an excellent
teacher; this is just one illustration. At the beginning of the class,
the teacher, Jim Minstrell, gives students a three-question quiz. One
of the questions reads as follows: "Under normal atmospheric conditions, an object is placed on a scale and the scale reads 10 pounds.
If the scale and the object were placed under a glass dome, and
all the air were removed from under the dome, what would the
scale read?"[3]

After fifteen minutes, Minstrell collects the quizzes and puts
some of the answers on the board; they range from fifteen to twenty
pounds to about zero. " 'Now let's hold off on attacking these
answers,' Minstrell announces. 'Rather, let's defend one or more of
them.' "[4] A number of students explain the reasoning behind their
answers. As Bruer describes it, "The most popular student response
is that the scale would read slightly less than 10 pounds. These arguments invoke facets involving density and buoyancy. John presents
the rationale: 'It's gonna be a little less than 10. You remember Bob
Beamon. He set a world record in the long jump at the Mexico City
Olympics. He jumped really far there because there is less air and it
is lighter and so everything weighs less.' "[5]

During the discussion, Bruer goes on to recount, "Minstrell is
strictly a facilitator, offering no facts, opinions, or arguments himself. He then encourages students to present counterarguments."[6]

After the discussion has run its course, Minstrell asks how the disagreement can be resolved. The students suggest setting up an experiment, an experiment Minstrell has already prepared for. Two students conduct the experiment in front of the class, and the result, a surprise to most of the students, is that the weight does not change when the air is removed from the container holding the scale and object. As the air is let back in, the students see that the weight doesn't change. "Minstrell asks, 'What does that tell us about gravity and air pressure?' 'Air pressure doesn't affect weight,' the students respond. They have started to correct a major misconception."[7]

If the "natural" approach is simply to inform students of information they don't yet know, Minstrell's performance is quite "unnatural"; at no point in the lesson is he conveying information. Minstrell knows what many "natural" teachers might not, that merely saying the words "Air pressure doesn't affect weight" or being able to plug values into a formula is not necessarily *understanding* the principles of physics. Minstrell realizes that understanding takes time, and he's willing to sacrifice coverage for understanding. His students don't get through the standard curriculum, while those of more "natural" teachers do. Notice that Minstrell's lesson appears highly congenial to my own aspirations for students. Minstrell is stimulating the students' capacity and disposition to solve physics problems. He's also giving them a feel for what constitutes evidence in physics and is modeling respect for that evidence.

What kind of knowledge lies behind Jim Minstrell's teaching? Minstrell has a deep knowledge of physics, but that is clearly not enough to make him an excellent teacher. He knows how intelligent but untutored students are likely to think about physics problems; he knows what misleading intuitions they are likely to harbor. Finally, he knows how to sustain the attention of a group of students.

Does Teaching Have a Scientific Basis?

Let us grant that Jim Minstrell is a master teacher. Is Minstrell's teaching knowledge similar to his knowledge of physics? Can it be codified, developed, and transmitted the way knowledge in physics is? In other words, is the teaching of physics itself a science? If it's not a science, is it a practical skill, like medicine, that has its *basis* in science?

Many students of the professions have noted that the prestige accorded professionals depends ultimately on the fact that they possess secrets—specialized knowledge to which laypeople have, at best, limited access. Still, the hope of discovering or inventing a "science" of teaching is not motivated simply by envy of the social status of doctors, lawyers, and architects. It is also fueled by the plausible idea that teaching might emulate the remarkable progress of scientifically grounded pursuits such as architecture, agriculture, and medicine. After all, medicine has had a head start of several hundred years while attempts to found a science of education are not even a hundred years old.

The idea is an attractive one, but certain considerations of a philosophical kind ought, at the very least, to moderate our expectations. Let's begin by noting two somewhat different ways in which scientific advances can enhance the effectiveness of a practical pursuit: by refining existing techniques and by suggesting novel ones.

One way in which a practical endeavor like agriculture or medicine improves through adopting scientific methods is by trying to link effects to their causes. Take medicine, for instance. New drugs are continually being discovered or developed in the laboratory, drugs whose beneficial effects must be demonstrated first on animals and then on humans in carefully designed clinical trials. Once a drug has been shown to be safe for human consumption, its efficacy must be tested. Typically, matched samples of patients are given either the experimental drug or a placebo, and the results are carefully monitored. If the new drug proves effective, it may then be tested against the currently preferred alternative to see which is most beneficial. Over time, the less effective treatments are gradually weeded out and the more effective ones are retained. The result is medical progress.

Much educational research for the last fifty years has followed this model but with few robust results or, more accurately, with few robust results that don't corroborate common sense. Here are the two most prominent findings as reported in the most recent *Handbook of Research on Teaching:* "One is that academic learning is influenced by amount of the time that students spend engaged in appropriate academic tasks. The second is that students learn more efficiently when their teachers first structure new information for them and help them relate it to what they already know."[8]

Why are the results of a half-century of increasingly sophisticated research on the relationship between a teacher's behavior in the classroom and learning outcomes not more impressive? A plausible explanation might be inferred from examining the analogy between medicine and teaching a bit more carefully.

Although no two patients and no two doctors are alike, it is often possible for the physician to select a treatment based on relatively little knowledge about the patient beyond the disease entity deemed responsible for the symptoms. Once a strep throat has been diagnosed, to take an admittedly easy case, the physician will typically prescribe penicillin, which has proved most effective against streptococci. Of course, this "drug of choice" may be contraindicated in cases where the patient has an allergy to penicillin. A host of variables may, however, safely be ignored. Neither gender nor ethnicity, neither temperament nor geographic location, neither personal preferences nor the general outlook of either the patient or the physician has to enter the treatment decision. Naturally, we all prefer a humane physician, but the penicillin will probably work no better if the doctor is a saint and no worse if he or she is a curmudgeon.

Now consider the classroom: Mr. Minstrell can't teach every group of students the same way. He is likely to take into account their age, maturity, gender, background knowledge, and educability. His approach, so successful in suburban Seattle, might fall flat in the inner city a half hour away. Here Minstrell's refusal to play the role of the conventional teacher might be taken as a sign of ineptness. It's also pretty clear that the approach successfully employed by Jim Minstrell might not be nearly as successful when it is used by another teacher with a different personality or teaching philosophy. A teacher with a very different personality might try and yet be unable to follow Minstrell's approach or might succeed in following his script with very different results. Our own experience in school confirms the notion that teachers are not interchangeable. What a particular teacher does well or poorly has much to do with the distinctive personality and background of that individual. The authors of the just-cited review of research on teaching, Jere E. Brophy and Thomas L. Good, realize that even the two research results reported above "must be qualified by grade level, type of objective, type of student, and other context factors."[9]

Note also that the hope of monitoring progress in any practical field, whether it be farming, medicine, or education, depends on identifying some unimpeachable standard of success. Consider the evaluation of progress in treating cancer, for example. Because cancer is such a deadly disease, mere survival in numbers of months or years is the generally agreed-upon yardstick, one that is hard to challenge. When it comes to judging physics education, the identification of such an unimpeachable standard becomes problematic. Earl Hunt, a researcher who works with Minstrell, is quoted by Bruer as saying, " 'From a traditional perspective one might argue that Minstrell's classes fail, because often students don't get through the standard curriculum.' "[10] There is no educational equivalent of survival. Identifying an unimpeachable standard of success in medicine is not, of course, always straightforward, but the problem is generally more tractable.

All of the above cautions notwithstanding, there is and always will be a place for this kind of scientific endeavor in efforts to improve teaching. If we were to abandon all efforts to systematically link the consequences of students' experiences in classrooms to their causes, we'd be forced to depend for guidance entirely on intuition, anecdote, and fable. These are valuable sources of illumination for the individual teacher in the classroom, but not a very reliable basis for designing policies to enhance the effectiveness of huge numbers of teachers. Keep in mind, though, that the degree to which teachers approach my three key aspirations is no easy thing to discover. Student achievement tests are very inadequate proxies for the dispositions and capacities that we hope to develop in students.

Can Cognitive Science Lead to Pedagogical Breakthroughs?

The most dramatic changes in technology have resulted, not from the continual refining of existing methods of doing things, but from the invention of totally new ones. Most of the inventions that have changed our lives depend on scientific discoveries. The word processor I'm writing on provides a convenient illustration. It was not invented by continual refinements and improvements to the typewriter. The invention of the word processor depended on a variety of discoveries in physics and mathematics, none of which resulted from scientists trying to create more efficient writing tools.

Now comes a central question: Can the development of a better understanding of the way people think and learn lead to powerful new approaches to teaching? John T. Bruer thinks this has *already* happened. In the article from which I quoted, he claims, "Cognitive science—the science of mind—can give us an applied science of learning and instruction. Teaching methods based on this research. . . are the educational equivalents of polio vaccine and penicillin. Yet few outside the educational research community are aware of these breakthroughs or understand the research that makes them possible."[11]

According to Bruer, "reciprocal teaching," an approach to teaching reading comprehension in elementary school developed by Annemarie Palincsar and Ann Brown,[12] exemplifies pedagogical breakthroughs based on advances in cognitive science.

Reciprocal teaching is based on the notion that expert readers avail themselves of four strategies to extract meaning from a text: summarizing, questioning, clarifying, and predicting. The core of the pedagogy has students in small groups take turns as leaders in employing these strategies. The group first reads the text silently, "then the assigned leader summarizes the passage, formulates a question that might be asked on a test, discusses and clarifies difficult points, and finally makes a prediction about what might happen next in the story. The teacher provides help and feedback tailored to the needs and abilities of the current leader. The student-listeners act as supportive critics who encourage the leader to explain and clarify the text."[13]

Is reciprocal teaching an educational equivalent of penicillin? According to Bruer, a controlled experiment tested reciprocal teaching against standard reading-skills instruction. After twenty days, "scores on daily comprehension tests improved to 72% for the reciprocal teaching group, versus 58% for the control group."[14] That constitutes a 24 percent improvement. In an early test of penicillin in 1941, five children were treated with 100 percent effectiveness. "All were at a stage where normal therapies had failed," according to the author of the article on penicillin in the *Encyclopedia of Medical History*.[15]

Most medical advances, of course, are not "miracles" like penicillin and the polio vaccine. A 24 percent improvement rate would be something to celebrate in many areas of medicine. Moreover, the fact that reciprocal teaching is not the miracle pedagogy trumpeted by Bruer does not limit the promise of yet-to-be-invented pedagogical innovations. Cognitive science is, after all, only about twenty years old. Note, however, that although you or I might never have invented reciprocal teaching, if we'd been asked to design a reading strategy based on our own sense of how we ourselves grapple with difficult texts, we might have come up with an approach that would not be entirely dissimilar. But no amount of introspection or survey of existing approaches to the treatment of infection seventy-five years ago would have led physicians to the discovery of penicillin.

I don't mean to take anything away from Palincsar and Brown's exemplary research and development efforts, nor to diminish the genuine advances in understanding represented by cognitive science, but inflated claims about educational "breakthroughs" such as Bruer's are, at the least, premature and likely to engender needless disappointment when they are not borne out. My skepticism regarding the potential pedagogical fruits of a still-young cognitive science is supported by two additional considerations.

One comes from history. This is not the first time that some educators and educational researchers have been swept off their feet by the contemporary fashion in academic psychology. A generation ago the behaviorists were claiming discovery of the Holy Grail—a theory of predicting and controlling human behavior. Many educators, even very sophisticated scholars, eagerly followed this Pied Piper. I recall a popular book by two prominent educational researchers, published in 1970, that announced a "development of major significance," the trend toward formulation of educational objectives, "not in the customary vague manner, but *in terms of measurable learner behavior.*"[16] James W. Popham and Eva Baker claimed then that "this development is one of the most important educational advances of the 1900's and signals a very significant attack upon the problems of education."[17]

It is instructive to note that the publication date of Popham and Baker's book, 1970, was fourteen years *after* a now-famous meeting of psychologists that, according to John Bruer, marked "the beginning of the cognitive revolution in psychology, a revolution that eventually replaced behaviorist psychology with a science of the mind."[18] Indeed, the model of mind that Bruer himself takes as authoritative, one invented by Allen Newell and Herbert Simon over twenty years ago, has itself come under serious challenge in recent years by those psychologists who favor a connectionist or "mental-models" view of cognitive processes.

My second basis for skepticism regarding the discovery of an educational equivalent of penicillin is related to a point I have been stressing throughout these pages, that what ultimately matters is what people are disposed to do and what they care about. Many, though admittedly not all, of the problems teachers face have to do with sustaining the focused attention of students on the subject at hand. The problem with many students who fall behind, whether in reading or physics, is that they cease to care and won't or can't pay attention. So the magic bullet that would do the most to revolutionize classrooms would be some utterly novel way of capturing the attention and commitment of children and adolescents. But what might that be? Rational appeals of all kinds have been tried by teachers for centuries. Systems of incentives that employ an enormous variety of rewards from grades and free time to money as well as penalties that range from detention to flogging have also been tried. Finally, efforts of all kinds to induce receptivity by making the classroom and its activities alluring and rewarding or by using innovative technologies—overhead projectors, language laboratories, film, computers, and, now, interactive videodiscs—have also been tried for as long as schools have existed. The notion that further advances in cognitive science will yield a pedagogical miracle drug that will finally capture students' commitment, while not impossible, has to strain our credulity.

What Educators Can Learn from Cognitive Science

While my discussion so far is aimed at lowering expectations for the discovery of the pedagogical "magic bullet," I'm appreciative of the lesson that cognitive science has for pedagogy. As I see it, though, that lesson is less of a discovery and more of a reminder. It concerns the way in which students' minds, and students themselves, should be understood: not as blank audiotapes, but as belonging to natives of an exotic culture who have their own ways of making sense of the world.

Since the analogy is mine (rather than Bruer's), let me explain what I mean. If students' minds are viewed as blank audiotapes, the job of the teacher is pretty straightforward—to transfer information onto them. That doesn't make the job of teaching easy, but it does make it rather straightforward: out of the vast storehouse of tapes that fill the teacher's mind, the specific information to be transferred must first be selected, then organized efficiently, and static must be minimized if the student is to receive a faithful copy. This is how Noelle Oxenhandler's lycée teachers viewed their task.

Now imagine that a university teacher of physics has identified a group of several hundred people from a preindustrial hunting and gathering culture, for example. Imagine that he has collected them in a modern university lecture hall and read to them the first week's lectures that he normally delivers to his freshman students (translated into their own language and with words coined where necessary). Assuming that these new "students" were paying attention and assuming that what they heard was even intelligible, I'm sure they would wonder about the lecturer's sanity—how could the teacher even entertain ideas that were so outlandish, so at variance with their own experience of the physical world. For these people have not only developed their own theories but know that those theories *work*; they and their ancestors, after all, have been finding their way in the jungle, navigating the streams and rivers, building durable shelters, and successfully tracking and hunting game for as long as they can remember.

The analogy between children and preindustrial peoples can be dangerous; I don't want to push it too far. What I'm trying to stress is that a successful teacher like Mr. Minstrell realizes that his students walk into the classroom with ideas about the physical world and with the ability to reason logically. As an intelligent teacher, he must use students' "native" ideas and their own powers of reasoning as a platform from which to begin reconstruction, not pretend that the students are blank tapes to be filled.

The reason I'm inclined to say that this "lesson" of cognitive science is more of a reminder than a discovery is that it is at least as old as Socrates. Socrates' students had to be relieved of their already well-established and functional beliefs about justice, holiness, knowledge, and the like if they were to make any progress; all Socrates had to go on were his students' abilities to reason about what they "knew," their curiosity, and their enjoyment of intelligent conversation. Palincsar and Brown understand, as does

Minstrell, as did Socrates, that students cannot learn to understand, cannot develop their capacities for further learning, and cannot come to care about evidence if their own ideas and their own intellectual capabilities remain unengaged.

Let's reassemble the pieces of the puzzle. Teaching is an everyday activity, one that we all engage in outside school classrooms with varying degrees of success. Efforts to place teaching on a scientific basis have not borne much fruit nor are they likely to, so I would argue, except insofar as they confirm what excellent pedagogues have always understood instinctively. It is doubtful that pedagogy progresses the way medicine does; this can be seen in the fact that most of us would be happy to have our adolescent children taught by Socrates, but quite unhappy to have them treated at the school clinic by Galen, the greatest physician of the ancient world.

At the outset, I said that teaching was an enormously demanding task. Now I've claimed that Socrates was just as effective as today's teachers, who are equipped with the results of a century's efforts to apply scientific methods to the study of human development and teaching and learning. Is there an inconsistency there? Can anyone with some knowledge in a subject be "dragged off the street," as the saying goes, and succeed as a classroom teacher? That does not follow, though it is an inference we are all too prone to make—the inference that if an activity doesn't have a scientific basis, then it is easy, requires no particular training, and merits little respect. Think about diplomacy, for example.[19] We're all natural diplomats, arranging "peace treaties" between our children, relatives, friends, work associates. There's no science of diplomacy so far as I know, nor does diplomacy depend on any science the way medicine depends on biology and chemistry. As with teachers, I'd guess that diplomats with a wide variety of personalities and styles of mediation have been and could be successful. Does that mean that anyone might be recruited to successfully negotiate a reconciliation between an estranged father and son, a contract dispute between a union and management, or a truce between warring factions or nations? I think not.

Perhaps some diplomats, like some teachers, are "born rather than made." It's silly, though, to think that teachers need to know only their own subject to succeed in teaching, as silly as to think that would-be diplomats need only background information on the disputes they are asked to resolve. It's highly unlikely that anyone who was ignorant of the complex nature and roots of the conflict between Israel and Egypt could have negotiated peace between those two nations, but mere information about the dispute and disputants won't, of itself, make one adept at settling disputes. It's just as unlikely that Mr. Minstrell could engender an understanding of gravity and air pressure without a mastery of physics, but such mastery is clearly not enough. What's needed in both cases is a grasp of the way one's "clients" are likely to think and react under various contingencies and a repertoire of strategies for eliciting cooperation, for helping these clients to overcome their instinct to walk out and abandon the proceedings. The teaching task in the precollege years is, if anything, more difficult, given the fact that teachers face, not a few courteous adults, but fairly large *groups* of potentially unruly children or adolescents whose presence is secured only through the coerciveness of the law. Keep in mind here that both my teaching vignettes, describing Mr. Minstrell's and Madame's classes, came from classrooms with relatively docile students. The challenge posed by resistant students is immeasurably more difficult.

Ultimately, the success or failure of mediation depends on what the parties to a dispute care about; ultimately, the success or failure of the teacher depends, likewise, on what her students come to care about. The personal "presence" of the teacher or mediator may count for a lot, inspire confidence and commitment, or only exacerbate an already difficult situation. At the end of the day, however, even the most heroic efforts by the most skilled practitioners may be to no avail if the "clients" are resistant.

Teaching and Policy

Does this mean that teachers don't make much of a difference? Imagine a school in which every science teacher was a Jim

Minstrell. Now imagine a school in which every science teacher was like the one who confronted Noelle Oxenhandler at the lycée: "In science class, we never touched a plant or stirred a solution or peered at an insect through a microscope. We sat silent in the dark watching slides of plankton, Louis Pasteur, and cowpox projected onto brown peeling plaster walls. . . . The teacher droned on in the background, but all I've retained is a single sentence, perhaps because it struck me as oddly heroic: 'Drop by drop, the urine forms itself in perpetuity.' "[20]

Do teachers make a difference? Of course they do, though we can't be sure how much and what kind of difference they make. In the real world of real schools, we hope that every student will have the opportunity to confront a Jim Minstrell, though we realize that there will be no way of avoiding the "Mesdames" (as their students are required to call them) described by Ms. Oxenhandler. The practical policy questions are these: how, if at all, can we retrain the Mesdames of this world to make them more like Jim Minstrell? How can we recruit and train more Jim Minstrells (and fewer Mesdames) and how can we keep them in the classroom?

I think it fair to say that we don't have an answer to the first question. We can see that Mr. Minstrell has, not only a much better understanding of the nature of science, but a very different conception of what he's up to as a teacher. For Madame to transform her pedagogy, she'd need a virtual conversion, one that transformed her basic understanding of her own mission. What makes that so difficult is not only her years of teaching the same way, but also her own experience as a student over the first quarter of her lifetime, to say nothing of her convictions—shared by her students, their parents, and the national examiners—that her current approach, while perhaps not exemplary, is at least sound. Her pedagogy is judged to be sound, at least in part, because it permits her to maintain control over a fairly large class of adolescent girls, control that might be jeopardized were she to invite students to move around the room, or to argue among themselves and to challenge her.

The second question, that of recruitment and training, also

admits of no ready answer. Of course, many will immediately say, "Pay more money to those entering the occupation," but there is no guarantee that paying another ten thousand dollars, say, to each entering teacher would attract only the Jim Minstrells of the world, and not those who just wanted a decent salary and two months off in the summer. In any case, prospects for such raises are unrealistic in a society where many people believe that teachers are already earning too much for the work they do.

Recent reformers, noting the ease with which candidates can obtain a teaching license, contend that professional teacher training needs to presuppose a bachelor's degree in the liberal arts if the occupation is to acquire the prestige of professions like law and medicine, where all training is at the postgraduate level. If those choosing occupations are motivated to any degree by the relationship between the cost of entering the occupation and the future income they can expect, this strategy would appear to be highly problematic. If the cost of entry into teaching rises relative to the cost of entry into other professions but earning power remains unchanged, shouldn't this prove a *deterrent* to the talented and ambitious? My own experience bears this out. I've taught a fair number of promising future teachers in an undergraduate certificate program who say that they would have opted for more prestigious professions such as law if entering teaching had required two years of postgraduate study.

The notion that we might enhance the prestige of teaching by raising standards for entering the occupation overlooks one of the peculiarities of teaching relative to other occupations, which is the way the definition of a minimally qualified practitioner varies with the supply and demand of teachers. When there is a shortage of physicians in some area of the country, medical students who have not completed their training are not designated as "provisional physicians" and invited to assume the role of physician. If these same areas are short of licensed teachers, however, pressure from parents will cause states to provide provisional teacher licenses to legally unqualified candidates. Alternative routes to licensing will then be made available to recruits who wish permanent positions. This stance is not unreasonable when a community might otherwise face the prospect of having sixty students in a class, a prospect that both parents and existing licensed teachers will reject out of hand. Efforts to raise the floor of what counts as a minimally qualified professional will begin to fail in those times and places where teacher shortages loom.

The practice of permitting technically unqualified teachers to serve in areas where there are severe shortages of qualified teachers is not as bankrupt as some teacher-educators make it out to be. "Teach for America," a program that puts graduates of elite liberal arts colleges into school classrooms with only a summer's teacher training, demonstrates what we intuitively knew, that some well-educated young people with no teacher training can perform as well in their first year of teaching as some graduates of professional teacher-preparation programs. Of course, some of these novices fail egregiously. It is, however, slightly misleading to claim that these liberal arts graduates have had only a few weeks of teacher preparation; they have, after all, observed scores of teachers doing their job for many *thousands* of hours. Since so few of the teachers they will have observed will have been Jim Minstrells, it's unlikely that they will model themselves after that kind of teacher, but the same is true, regrettably, of many of their counterparts at traditional teacher training institutions.

Let me be clear here; I do not join those critics who glibly say that all would be well in our schools if we only abolished teacher training institutions and focused our efforts on mastery of subject matter. I ask those who sympathize with these critics to perform the following thought experiment: imagine the average holder of a Ph.D. degree in physics or literature. Now plunk her down in a classroom of fourth graders and ask her to teach reading or science. What is the probability that she would model her pedagogy on that of Palincsar and Brown or Jim Minstrell? Not very high, I'd wager.

One approach deserves mention that both makes it more likely that the Jim Minstrells will remain in teaching and encourages the

Mesdames to improve as well. This is an approach that, while not without its problems, is gaining credibility in many states and school districts: giving the Jim Minstrells additional prestige and remuneration and a reduced teaching load to allow them to undertake additional responsibilities in the continuing education of their peers. Differentiated staffing, as it's called, is a sensible idea from the pedagogical point of view, though it does run the danger of exacerbating the inequalities that will be discussed in Chapter Seven, with wealthy districts outbidding poorer ones for "master" or "lead" or "board-certified" teachers. Differentiated staffing, in conjunction with other measures designed to establish a more collaborative work culture, merits our support. I'll have a bit more to say about this in the next chapter.

In the absence of decisive evidence showing that one approach to the recruitment, training, or certification of teachers is more effective than another, our decentralized educational system, with its myriad teacher training institutions and fifty different sets of licensing regulations, is not necessarily a danger, though it is a deterrent to geographic mobility. Why put all our eggs in one basket when we have no sound basis for selecting baskets? Many reformers and commentators are uncomfortable with the lack of standardization and the free-for-all quality of the whole enterprise of teacher training and teacher licensing, but let's remind ourselves that the Mesdames who imprinted such unfavorable memories on Ms. Oxenhandler were all products of a highly centralized and standardized educational system.

It is difficult for me to identify any feasible set of policies that I could confidently predict would substantially reduce the likelihood that the next generation of students would have to face their share of Mesdames as they made their way through twelve years of compulsory schooling. This may not necessarily be the disaster we might suppose it to be, however. I know nothing of the biography of Ms. Oxenhandler except that she attended the French lycée for a year, an experience that consisted of "moments of drama in a tedium so extreme that it was—for me—almost exotic."[21] I suspect, though I do not know, that her little reminiscence in the *New Yorker* is not her first published piece. Presumably, her ability and propensity to keep on learning were not destroyed by that dismal lycée experience. How do we explain her resilience?

Here, we can only speculate. Perhaps the native disposition to learn, once it has been ignited by talented teachers, is difficult to extinguish by mediocre ones. Perhaps, despite Ms. Oxenhandler's recollection of extreme tedium, the shortcomings of the Mesdames were not total liabilities from the educational point of view. How might this be possible? Perhaps the plodding persistence exhibited by the lycée teachers reinforced a patience and tenacity in some students that would stand them well in subsequent studies.

The defects of traditional, "natural" pedagogy, teaching as telling, have been emphasized by progressive educators since Jean-Jacques Rousseau. In the main, these criticisms are well taken, and I agree with them. Perhaps, though, traditional pedagogy has some hidden virtues, or perhaps its vices are not as pernicious as progressives believe. Keep in mind that almost all the creative contributors to the arts and sciences over the last two hundred years, including the most ardent critics of traditional pedagogy, were products of traditional schools. This is evidence that progressive educators committed to respecting evidence cannot overlook. What are we to make of it?

John Dewey said many years ago that the effects of an educational experience are not borne on its face. The fruits of diverse pedagogies are found, ultimately, not in the demeanor of students in the classroom, not in the achievement test scores taken at the end of the semester, but in the enduring attitudes and dispositions that they foster. Perhaps all of us, progressives and conservatives alike, know less about the conditions needed for these fruits to ripen than we would like to believe. Systematic investigation can help us learn more, though if the argument of this chapter is right, hopes for magic pedagogical bullets are illusory.[22]

Chapter Five

Accountability

Critics of American public education have all too successfully sold us on the notion that American public schools are hopelessly inadequate and inefficient, perhaps the major cause of America's deteriorating position relative to Japan. For example, the achievement of students in science and mathematics is typically portrayed as abysmal, and schools in major cities are regularly depicted as educational disaster zones. It is not hard to find hard facts and figures to support such assertions, yet other facts and figures paint a rather different picture. Take a couple of examples: for the years 1989–1993, over 70 percent of all Nobel prizes in four sciences went to Americans; *none* went to Japanese.[1] In 1994, more than a quarter of the 40 finalists (chosen from 1,645 entrants from every state) in the prestigious Westinghouse Science Talent Search attend New York City public schools. No New York City winner attends a private school.[2]

Regardless of whether we agree with the naysayers or the revisionists about the performance of American students, the perception that schools lack accountability is widespread. *For what, how,* and *to whom* should they be held accountable? These questions are difficult to separate and surprisingly difficult to answer. In this chapter, I'll focus on the first two questions, deferring the last question till the next chapter. The questions of how and for what to hold schools accountable may be posed at the level of the individual classroom, at the level of the school or school district, and even at the state level. Let's begin with the classroom.

Teacher Accountability

Teachers, whether they work in private or public schools, are employees who are paid a salary for doing a particular job—teaching fourth grade, or remedial reading, or high school physics. No one denies that teachers ought to be answerable for what they do, but what does that mean? On the most basic level it means that they may be asked and ought to be able to explain and defend a particular action—sending a student out of the room, assigning a controversial text, permitting students to work together in teams, scheduling a test for a particular day, or whatever. It is understood here that certain kinds of answers, such as "I just felt like it" or "That's how we've always done it," are insufficient, that a satisfying rationale will connect the action to some putative educational benefit to the group or to an individual student. I trust that this is acceptable, so far as it goes, but does it go far enough? Most will think that it does not. Many will think that teachers need to be held accountable for *results*, and some would go so far as to propose that teacher remuneration be dependent on those results. Often identified with the world of the business corporation, this view has at least a superficial plausibility, and it deserves examination.

Imagine a corporate sales manager's view of accountability: "I know that both successful and unsuccessful salespeople can explain and defend the actions they take. Of course, I'll listen to attempts to explain failure, but when all is said and done, what the company needs is sales, not explanations. The interest in results is reflected in our reward structure: successful salespeople get rewarded with commissions, while the unsuccessful earn only a basic salary. Continued failure to make sales will probably result in the loss of the job itself. Such a reward structure may appear heartless, but a company that rewarded its entire sales force equally—regardless of performance—wouldn't stay in business long."

When this stance is transferred to the schoolroom, it looks like this: "Teachers are contracted to teach reading or physics to particular groups of kids. If a particular group of students succeeds beyond what could have been expected, their teacher deserves remuneration beyond that of her colleague whose students' performance is only mediocre. If her students' achievement falls below expectations for such a group—and there are no mitigating circumstances—perhaps she, like the inept salesperson, is in the wrong kind of work. Teachers may find this policy heartless, but should kids' learning—their futures, perhaps—be sacrificed in order to spare the feelings of incompetent teachers?"

This stance is anathema to most teachers, but does anything besides protection of their own job security lie behind their revulsion? Teachers will immediately point out that the success of their students ultimately depends on others' efforts—on the kind of support they receive from the school's administrators and parents and, most important, on the students' own motivation, over which the teachers exercise only limited influence. "You can lead a horse to water . . ." as the proverb goes.

This is true, but it does not constitute a satisfactory objection to the result-oriented accountability. The salesperson's success is also dependent on others—on the technical and administrative resources available to the sales force and, finally, on the customer's interest in making the purchase. There *is* an important difference between the two cases, however. If the teacher's students fail—setting aside the meaning of success and failure for a moment—there is probably no way of knowing whether another teacher could have succeeded in her place. It's possible that no teacher could have done much better with that group of students. It's also possible that the same teacher could have done creditably with a different group of students. In most sales contexts, several vendors compete for the same customer. If company A fails to make the sale, it's because the customer made a decision to buy from company B. Assuming that a company's products are competitive as reflected in sales made by other salespeople, we can, at least over time, plausibly assign responsibility for lack of success to the performance of an individual salesperson. Such assignment of responsibility is extremely difficult in the world of the classroom. If the success or failure of students can't be reliably linked to the performance of the teacher, wouldn't any reward structure that makes the teacher's rewards contingent on student performance seem arbitrary and rightly be resented by teachers?

Student Achievement as a Basis for Teacher Accountability

There is another difficulty with result-oriented accountability, a difficulty that emerges once we ask ourselves what results we're going to focus on. One answer, the most obvious and the most tempting to many, is student performance on examinations. Is this a suitable basis for teacher accountability? Let's make the discussion more concrete by focusing on an actual examination question, one taken from a pilot study by the National Assessment of Educational Progress, a government agency entrusted with assessing the intellectual capabilities of students as they move through their schooling:

> Usually your heart beats regularly at a normal rate when you are at rest. Suppose someone asks you the following questions:
> * Does your heart rate go up or down when you exercise?
> * How much does your heart rate change when you exercise?
> * How long does the effect last?
> Think about what you would do to find answers to the questions above. What type of experiment would you design to answer the questions? Assume that you have the following equipment available to use: an instrument to measure your heart rate (such as a pulse meter), a stop watch, and some graph paper. Briefly describe how you might go about finding answers to these questions.[3]

I choose this question because it does not call for a mere recital of facts recalled from the textbook or from the teacher's lecture. The question appears well suited to finding out whether students understand how to find evidence of a particular kind and bring it to bear on a question they have little information about, certainly an important attainment from my own point of view. Notice that, as with any test question, this one draws on a variety of capabilities: the student must be able to read with understanding (for example, words like *effect*); must have mastered certain concepts such as "rate," "change of rate," and "designing an experiment"; must be able to grasp how a stopwatch or graph paper would be helpful tools; and so on. Perhaps most important and most subtle, the student has to grasp that what is being asked is not what the relationship between heart rate and exercise is but *how to find out* what it is.

I believe that answers to examination questions like this one would tell us quite a bit about students' intellectual sophistication, but what would they tell us about the teacher's performance? That would depend on what the teacher—let's call her Ms. Lehrer, a ninth grade science teacher—has taught the students as it relates to that question. Suppose that this is a semester course in earth science and things like heart rate are not part of the syllabus, and suppose that a particular group of students does very poorly on this question and, of course, on others like it. Can we hold Ms. Lehrer accountable and penalize her accordingly? That would appear to be very unfair to her. I could imagine her arguing as follows: "My students are, regrettably, not very bright, but I've taught them a lot about the earth over an entire semester. Now you come in, give them a question that tests their general intelligence rather than any of the specific material I've taught them, a test they flunk—and you want to hold *me* responsible? That makes about as much sense as blaming a driver for an auto accident that was caused by a faulty part."

Let's ask ourselves under what circumstances Ms. Lehrer would accept the students' responses to this question as a test of her *own* competence. First of all, long before the semester began, she would expect to have a pretty clear idea of the kinds of questions and the range of topics on which the students would be examined. If she did not have access to such information, she could hardly be blamed for not preparing her students to take the examination. Second, she would expect to be judged only against teachers facing a comparable challenge. A way would have to be found to match her students only with those demonstrating similar levels of prior achievement and comparable resources outside school, which is no easy task. Even if all this were done, Ms. Lehrer would still be very uneasy, for her evaluation remains dependent on the students' demonstration of competence in domains, such as reading and writing, that fall outside science, the subject she was ostensibly hired to teach. But assume that Ms. Lehrer was satisfied with the responses to all these concerns, and assume that the evaluation was important to her. How would we expect her to behave?

She could be expected to focus all her efforts on training students to answer questions like the ones that would be on the test. Any detours to topics not on the test would be at best a risky diversion. Of course, Ms. Lehrer couldn't be sure of the precise questions that would be asked, but she could be pretty sure, for example, that students would have to describe experiments that would yield evidence about the relationships between interdependent phenomena, or else she would never accept the students' performance as a measure of her own success. If a substantial reward or penalty depended on the success of her slower students, Ms. Lehrer would do everything she could to give them formulas to follow in answering such questions. She'd try as hard as she could to train the students to formulate responses that were as swift as possible lest they waste precious time and answer fewer questions. (An algebra teacher I had in high school in New York State—where students are required to pass state Regents examinations—followed exactly this policy and was considered an outstanding teacher because her students scored so high on the exam.) If Ms. Lehrer had a couple of students who, after all this preparation, still didn't understand, she might try to have them transferred into special education or simply recommend that they stay home the day of the exam. If there were a way of getting a peek at the questions beforehand, she might be tempted to do that in order to pass along some clues, if not actual answers, to the students.

I haven't invented any of these strategies. They come from news reports and studies of teachers' responses to "high-stakes" tests. The irony of the whole scenario is, of course, that a test originally designed to see how well students use their minds in novel situations is liable to become a device to focus the teacher's efforts on training students to offer routine responses to predictable stimuli.

Using student test scores to evaluate teachers necessarily distorts the educational process in such a way that the key aspirations identified in Chapter Two take a back seat to other, in my view less laudable, objectives. Let me elaborate. Recall that I identified the propensity to keep on learning and to respect evidence as key aspirations for students. These are dispositions that reveal themselves in the way young people respond to intellectual and other challenges—they are not competencies to be demonstrated on an examination.

Still, as I pointed out, these dispositions can only be formed through the development of particular skills and understanding. Teachers can easily test for the extent to which such particular attainments have been developed; indeed, they must, if only to find out where their teaching needs to be improved. But once student test scores become the *principal* target, teachers will inevitably focus on the performance of their students *now*, ignoring and possibly subverting the development of the dispositions that will serve them well *later*. Consider an analogy from the world of competitive sports. Coaches often maintain, no doubt correctly, that athletics can help build character, nurturing virtues such as the ability to subordinate personal desires for the good of the team, to abide by rules laid down for the good of all, to show courage in adversity and grace in victory and defeat. But, as we all know, the development of these character traits is imperiled when winning becomes, in the phrase attributed to former football coach Vince Lombardi, not everything, but the *only* thing. Under those conditions, a propensity to chicanery, hypocrisy, and ruthlessness is more likely to be developed.

Assessing Teacher Performance
to Achieve Accountability

Structuring teachers' rewards on the basis of their students' performance risks corrupting the educational process in ways I find unacceptable. Let's consider an alternative approach: evaluating the actual work of teachers without trying to assess student achievement. Teacher performance in the classroom can be evaluated as can teachers' plans for that performance. Indeed, this is the customary way in which novice teachers are judged to determine whether they deserve permanent positions. Yet any proposal to make remuneration (or other rewards or penalties) dependent on such evaluations will meet stiff resistance from teachers. Why?

Teachers are afraid that the process will be polluted by workplace politics, in which favors are exchanged and friends are rewarded by friends, as well as by the more public politics in which the propriety of airing certain topics or points of view in front of public school children is contested. Here, it seems to me that teachers' fears are well placed, not because school administrators are so easily corrupted but because impartial judgment is virtually impossible to secure.

A comparison with medicine can prove illuminating. In medicine, the basis for judgments of competence and incompetence is much more firmly established. If, for example, a patient presents symptoms that indicate the need for certain tests and those tests are not ordered; or if the doctor's diagnosis errs by failing to take account of a symptom that has been reported; or if the medication ordered for a particular condition, though normally appropriate, would be contraindicated given additional information known to be at hand; then the doctor can be held accountable for these deviations from standard practice, even though the proper action would not have guaranteed the patient's recovery.

In teaching, on the other hand, once we set aside fairly egregious cases of negligence or misconduct such as dating or hitting a student, failing to plan lessons, or consuming alcohol on the job, to take a few examples, it is hard to achieve consensus on what *ought* to constitute standard practice, deviations from which should be sanctioned. Of course, some generalizations hold in most classroom situations, such as one cited in the last chapter ("academic learning is influenced by amount of the time that students spend engaged in *appropriate academic tasks*")[4] but what counts as an appropriate academic task will depend heavily on situational factors that are hard to evaluate objectively, the characteristics of the students, the teacher's own agenda, and so on. A plausible defense of virtually any pedagogical practice can be mounted, and we must not forget that some of the best as well as some of the worst teachers deviate substantially from conventional practice. Remember also that a teacher's own behavior as well as that of his students is influenced by an evaluator's presence, so that unless the evaluator is prepared to visit fairly regularly, she cannot say with any confidence that she's seeing the lesson that would be enacted in her absence.

There's little doubt in my own mind that Mr. Minstrell is a better teacher than Madame, but can we convincingly *demonstrate* (to her and her union) that she is unworthy of the raise everyone at her school expects? I doubt it. She does, after all, conform to standard pedagogical practice and her students may perform no worse on the year-end exam than those of her more innovative neighbor.

I don't mean to deny that there are some clearly incompetent teachers in our public schools, teachers whose retention year after year depends not on the problems associated with identifying incompetence, but on the strength of teachers' unions in protecting their own regardless of incompetence. What I am denying is the likelihood that an impartial performance evaluation system could provide the basis for allocating differential rewards to teachers.

This leaves us in an uncomfortable position. We have criticized the most obvious alternatives for holding teachers accountable; must we then simply tolerate inept or lazy teachers? Let's distinguish two problems: (1) what to do about the obviously incompetent and (2) how to enhance the performance of teachers who, while not inept, are simply going through the motions, having lost the disposition to keep on learning their craft. The first problem is the one that is most vexing to administrators, and to parents when their children get stuck with an irresponsible or ineffective teacher, but there is no difficulty, either practical or theoretical, in identifying the truly incompetent. If we admit that truly inept or irresponsible teachers are actually rare, the second problem is arguably the more important. To my way of thinking, both problems are connected to an often-noted feature of teachers' work—that performance is invisible to everyone but the students themselves.

Teachers are notoriously leery of observing other teachers or permitting colleagues, even close friends, to observe their own teaching. This strong ethos of classrooms as private sanctuaries clearly deprives teachers of opportunities to see others in action and to receive counsel from colleagues who've overcome or at least faced similar problems. In my view, the perception that teachers are not sufficiently accountable is closely connected to the way their workplace is structured to prevent their being able to benefit from the successes and failures of their peers. Consequently, I would propose measures designed to end teachers' isolation. This is hardly new and, of course, much easier said than done. If Madame is to visit Jim Minstrell's classroom (or vice versa), she will need a free period or someone will have to teach her students while she's gone. Such logistical problems are very real, but they should not be allowed to block the development of what I'd call a new pedagogical culture—that is, a context in which the daily problems of classroom teaching can become shared problems and their solutions shared solutions.

The new pedagogical culture should not be confined within particular schools. Teachers need to have regular contact with peers in other institutions from whom they can learn as well as teach. Collaborative networks of teachers who come together to work on the pedagogical challenges facing them are not a new idea. Systematic evidence from studies conducted by researcher Milbrey W. McLaughlin demonstrates that such collaboratives do make a difference.[5]

Nurturing teacher collaboration, within and between schools, must be at the heart of efforts to improve accountability.

Accountability of Schools and School Systems

Most of the current demand for accountability is not focused on the single classroom but on larger educational units—the school, the school district, and the state. The latter two are the jurisdictional units with legal responsibility for schooling. Here is where broader policy issues are decided, and here is where taxpayer dollars are collected and their use determined. Inasmuch as all public agencies are ultimately accountable to the voters, we might argue that school systems are *already* accountable. Boards of education are normally elected by the voters, and state education departments are typically headed by a state superintendent who is elected or, if not elected, appointed by a governor who is elected. Voters often do turn out incumbent school board members or state superintendents when they're unhappy with the direction in which their school district or state is going.

Critics argue, however, that parents have every reason to be dissatisfied with the public schools, that their children are not getting the education they deserve, and that schools are both ineffective and inefficient. (*Effectiveness* pertains to educational quality, *efficiency* to quality as it relates to cost.) The intense conviction in some quarters that schools lack accountability is based on the perception that schools are taking an ever larger share of the public purse without delivering a better educational service. Thomas Sowell expresses this sentiment when he writes, "Looking at money input and educational output over time makes the education establishment's claims of inadequate financing look even more ridiculous. The period of declining test scores was also a period when expenditures on education were rising—rising not only in money terms but also in real terms, allowing for inflation. . . . In over-all per pupil expenditure, the U.S. ranks near the top, even though the performance of its students often ranks at or near the bottom."[6]

What new means of accountability might this kind of dissatisfaction give rise to? Two broad approaches have been proposed.
One involves identifying the desired educational outcomes and
standards of performance beforehand, giving schools and school systems a certain time period within which to reach them, measuring
those outcomes at the end of the predetermined time, and then providing incentives for success and penalties for failure. This is the
approach that was adopted recently by the state of Kentucky in a
massive reform effort initiated in 1990. The second approach gives
parents much more power by permitting them to choose their children's schools, either from among all schools or from among public
schools. My task here is not to explore all the advantages and liabilities of these approaches, but rather to discuss some of their
underlying assumptions.

The first approach depends ultimately on some way of assessing
the sought-after outcomes. Since we're dealing with entire schools
or school districts that enroll hundreds if not thousands of students,
it is clear that some means must be found to aggregate and compare
the performance of large numbers of institutions and students. This
requirement leads inevitably to the search for quantifiable data. In
Kentucky, according to *Education Week*, attendance rates, dropout
rates, and student scores on tests in grades four, eight, and twelve
will be combined into an *accountability index*, a number that will
provide the basis for rewards or sanctions.[7] We have already seen
that the three key aspirations I formulated for all students—that
they come to respect evidence and enhance both their capacity and
their desire to keep on learning—are difficult to assess, let alone to
measure. Performance on achievement tests may or may not be a
reasonable proxy for what we should really be after, but let's ignore
that problem for a moment, keeping in mind the difficulties identified in the previous section. The design of the accountability
index and the reward system geared to it appear to be mere technical problems, but they are not. Consider the following set of questions, adding in each case the additional question of who has
authority to answer it.

First, the index will aggregate scores on attendance rates and achievement scores, to name just two of the criteria. How much will each be weighted? If the dropout score does not count very much, a policy that encourages weak students to drop out rather than fail the achievement tests might be advisable. If the dropout rate counts a great deal relative to the achievement tests, it might be prudent to divert some investment in raising the average level of academic achievement to dropout-prevention programs, even if those programs do little to improve the academic performance of students who are vulnerable to dropping out.

Second, how is the threshold for rewards and penalties to be set? Is there to be a uniform basis for success or is the standard to vary with the background of the students. If the standard is uniform, we appear to be rewarding and penalizing schools with no regard to factors that we know play a substantial role in students' likelihood of academic success. On the other hand, if we set different thresholds in different social contexts, we appear to be giving children from less fortunate circumstances the message that less is expected of them academically, something we surely don't want to do, especially in the current climate, in which teachers' expectations are believed to be so decisive.

Third, is the index of student achievement needed to get rewards or avoid sanctions to be a *mean* score of all students taking the test, or a percentage of scorers that reach some *minimal threshold*, or the average achievement *gain* from the beginning to the end of the year? If it's the first, then the school has to consider the best way of reaching the required mean. A triage approach might be most effective. Such an approach would ignore both the students who can get a high score without extra help and those who are the riskiest investment—that is, those who even with extra help might not get passing scores—and focus efforts on the students whose scores are most likely to be boosted by a concerted effort. If the second option, reaching a minimal threshold, is chosen, a prudent policy would be to focus instructional efforts on the students who are likely to fail, leaving the most academically advanced students to their own devices as much as is feasible. If the third option, the average gain score, is chosen, a prudent (unofficial) policy would be to see to it that student performance on the initial test is low, making the subsequent gains appear to be very large. In this case, too, if the average gain score is to be the basis for rewards and penalties, a triage policy may be advisable.

Finally, consider the notion of rewards and penalties in this context. Presumably the thinking behind the reward structure is to sustain the efforts of successful schools and enhance the efforts of failing schools. But would such rewards and penalties actually do that? Suppose that the reward were five hundred dollars for every teacher in the successful school and the threat that of losing one's job in a school in which student achievement fell. The rewards might well boost the morale of teachers in the successful schools, but what would be the effect of the threatened penalty on the teachers in the failing schools? Any successful teachers would seek to transfer out to a successful school, thus increasing the inequalities. The remaining teachers, assuming that they were not too demoralized, would mount a strategy to avoid being penalized. It's not too hard to imagine that they would adopt the same kind of strategy as that of a football coach who is faced with the prospect of losing his job unless he has a winning season. I leave it to readers to decide if the resulting educational climate is what they would want for their children.

Suppose that despite every effort, a school fails to improve and its teachers are discharged. Is there a pool of qualified and motivated teachers willing to take over the school, or will teachers who are succeeding at other schools have to be compelled to teach there? Notice how different this situation is from one in which, say, a highway buckles and a veteran contractor loses its contract with the state. Here, presumably, competitors are able and only too eager to take on the additional work.

The gist of the preceding argument is this: an accountability system of the kind I've described is intended to redirect schools' or school districts' efforts. First, I asked whether those new efforts were going to be directed to educationally laudable aspirations or to quantifiable targets that would satisfy the need for accounting. The two are not necessarily inconsistent, of course, but exclusive focus on the latter is likely to jeopardize the former. Second, I asked if the redirected efforts would focus on *all* children or only on those needed to satisfy the accountants. I suggested the latter. It is likely that schools would neglect either the children whose accomplishments were already evident or those in whom the investment of time and energy is riskiest. Consider an analogy: suppose that an accountability system for hospitals were to go into effect based on patients' length of stay and the results, on average, of a standard blood test given at the time of discharge. What would the consequences be? The institutions' primary focus would be on attaining the proper blood levels for the test, maybe by giving a particular drug rather than by curing the underlying pathology. Efforts might well be redirected away from the sickest patients, those whose blood could not be brought into the normal range; and patients who needed an extra day or two to recuperate might be sent home prematurely. In designing systems of accountability, it is not enough to have a plausible surrogate for hard-to-measure aspirations. Redirecting energy to satisfy the accounting system must actually constitute progress toward satisfying the aspirations.

Let's turn now to the alternative approach to accountability, empowering the "customer" by introducing markets into the educational system. This approach is based on the plausible idea that without competitors, government monopolies have little incentive to increase effectiveness or efficiency. It is supported by the observation that affluent parents already exercise choice over their children's schooling by choosing their residence or choosing private schooling. Only the financially less fortunate are stuck with the schools to which their children are assigned, so the argument goes, and those schools have no incentive to improve.

It is hard to argue with the notion that if schools had to compete for children, they would work to become more "customer-friendly." Pleasing parents is not necessarily the same as providing a sound education for children, however. Consider restaurants: there is little doubt that fast-food chains like McDonald's and Pizza Hut have designed settings and menus that are satisfying to parents and children alike, yet dieticians have repeatedly noted the nutritional deficiencies of the food served at these establishments. Just as such fast-food establishments try to attract customers with gimmicks of all kinds that have nothing to do with the food they serve, so might schools use similar approaches to attract parents and children. Of course, parents who are aware of the nutritional deficiencies of most fast-food restaurants limit their patronage, but less well-educated parents do not. Educational markets would be attractive to parents who have the savvy and the leisure to make the wisest choices for their children. Parents who lack the time and those with the least experience in judging educational institutions would, on the other hand, be the ones most likely to be taken advantage of, just as they so often are in other markets.

Critics like Sowell argue that "the responses of the educational establishment to the academic deficiencies of their students today include (1) secrecy, (2) camouflage, (3) denial, (4) shifting the blame elsewhere, and (5) demanding more money."[8] Suppose that schools had to compete for students and the schools that could not attract a sufficient clientele faced the possibility of going out of business. Would this create an incentive for them to disclose unpleasant facts about themselves and the performance of their students? Prior to consumer protection legislation, did American auto manufacturers competing for customers disclose facts about the safety of their products? Whatever inclination educators have to conceal their failures would probably only be reinforced if they had to compete for students. Several months after I first wrote this sentence, an article in the *New York Times* corroborated my concern.[9] The article reported that Education Alternatives, a private company that manages public schools for profit, admitted that it had overstated the academic progress of students attending the schools it manages in Baltimore. Subsequent to the company's acknowledgment, its stock plummeted.

Another reason to doubt that introducing markets will substantially improve schools is the fact that although critics like Sowell denounce public education with great vigor, most parents are satisfied with the schools their children attend. According to the latest Phi Delta Kappa/Gallup poll of attitudes toward their local public schools, 56 percent of public school parents give the schools an A or B grade compared to 37 percent of non–public school parents and 44 percent of those with no children in school.[10] In fact, the vehemence of critics like Sowell derives in part from what they believe is misguided parental complacency about the schooling their children are receiving. Under a market system, parents might possibly drive down the *cost* of schooling, since everyone is happy to save money, but there is little basis for thinking that on average, parents would drive up the *quality*.

Despite the fact that the two approaches to accountability are so different—one, in a sense, increasing the power of government to regulate quality and the other reducing the role of government—the second approach would probably be vulnerable to some of the liabilities we found in the first one. No system of education markets can operate fairly or efficiently in the absence of accurate information about the alternatives. In addition to information about the educational process (the student-teacher ratio, the size of the library, and so on), it is reasonable to suppose that parents would want information about the schools' educational "outputs," scores on tests being the most likely index of comparison. It is likely that as educational markets become more popular, attention to such output measures will increase, with all the attendant problems I mentioned above.

Is Accountability Necessary?

Given the aspirations for education that I've articulated, and given the difficulties with mechanisms of accountability that I've identified, many might argue that current talk and efforts to make schools and school systems more accountable are not only misguided but dangerous. I sympathize with this way of thinking, but it should not allow us to evade the problem. School systems are continually demanding more funding. Figures from the federal government's *Digest of Education Statistics 1992* reveal that real expenditures per pupil between 1959–60 and 1989–90 did rise by 206 percent.[11] As demands for school spending rise, so do demands from other public agencies involved in meeting legitimate if not indispensable societal needs embracing everything from AIDS testing to economic development. Raising taxes is simply not politically feasible. If schools get more taxpayer funds, public health or welfare or higher education or the criminal justice system or highway maintenance must get less.

No doubt some feel uneasy assigning dollar values to the outputs of schooling, but they should and probably do feel equally uncomfortable thinking about health or social services in terms of efficiency. Taxpayers cannot be expected to continue to fund schools if they perceive an absence of accountability. What needs to be done is to address the public's right to know what's going on in schools without subverting the educational process itself. How can this be done?

Entrusted with guiding the educational system, the elected and appointed school boards and the citizens they represent have a right to information that will help them determine whether the schools are actually implementing the policies they've designed to enhance the education of their children. Educational policies at district and state levels embrace many different concerns, among them the allocation of funds to individual schools; assignment of students to individual schools and to classes within those schools (these policies deal with matters such as tracking, inclusion of children with disabilities, and desegregation); procedures to be followed with truant or unruly students and with students whose academic progress falls below minimal expectations for promotion; and the number of interviews with guidance counselors students can expect to have as they progress through their schooling.

School districts have policies concerning the qualifications for hiring and tenure in the school system, including the kinds of evaluation that teachers can expect; the assignment and transfer of teachers to individual schools; class size and teacher workload; the kinds of plans and logs teachers are expected to keep and procedures for dealing with teachers whose performance falls below those expectations; and the kinds of demands teachers and students may place on each other—for example, the number of essays or themes students will be expected to write in high school English classes and the kinds of feedback teachers can be expected to provide.

The public has a right to know both what these policies are *and* the extent to which they are complied with. A school "report card" providing detailed facts and figures on the degree to which legitimate mandates are actually followed should be published regularly in the newspaper. When teachers or school administrators evade or ignore legitimate policies, they should be held accountable, and in the absence of extenuating circumstances, they should be subject to disciplinary action.

This kind of accountability will not, of course, guarantee student academic achievement, but in the nature of the case nothing can guarantee that, any more than a hospital can guarantee that all its patients will go home cured. The public does have a right to reasonable *indicators* of children's academic achievement. It has a right to expect that teachers and students whose achievement is noteworthy are recognized for their success and that schools with severe problems are given the resources and personnel needed to turn their fortunes around. For all the reasons mentioned above, however, it would be a grave mistake to try to convert achievement indicators into objectives for which schools and teachers should be held accountable.

Ultimately, students' progress toward realizing the key aspirations will depend on the quality and motivation of their teachers, the resources they have to do their job, and, of course, the efforts the students put forth. Is it possible to assess the performance of schools and students with respect to my aspirations? As I've said, this will not be easy, but instruments designed to assess dispositions, attitudes, and preferences do exist. Since everyone attends school, it is difficult to study its impact. We have no control groups of people who don't go to school with which to compare school attenders. Still, efforts should be undertaken to collect evidence concerning the impact of various kinds of schooling on adult character and commitments.

Although citizens are entitled to information concerning what schools are actually doing with their tax monies, the information in an annual report cannot be expected to offer teachers any more guidance in their daily work with children than the report of a rise or fall in length of patient stay in city hospitals would offer the practicing nurse or physician. The best way for teachers to see a need to redirect their efforts and to develop some means of doing so is by watching colleagues they admire and receiving constructive suggestions from their peers. I return, therefore, to the point I made earlier. The best way to enhance the performance of schools is to transform the culture of teaching by transforming teachers' workplaces.

Chapter Six

Authority

It is time to confront a question posed at the beginning of the previous chapter: To whom should schools be held accountable? The answer is clear: to those who have the legitimate authority to make educational decisions. But who is that? The answer here is not only less clear but contested. American tradition is divided between a historic commitment to public schooling, which suggests accountability to the citizenry as a whole, and a recurring undercurrent of fear that public schools will trample on the rights of individual parents. The latter position is articulated most explicitly by libertarians, advocates of minimal governmental intervention in the lives of citizens, who wish to assign authority and responsibility for children's education exclusively to their own parents.

The strategy I'll pursue in the chapter is this: I'll begin by formulating and defending the libertarian view as strongly as I can, because it is this view that is most threatening to the justification of a system of public schools. I'll move then to identifying the weaknesses in the libertarian position and the extent to which those weaknesses move us toward defending public schooling. I'll then be in a position to explain why and under what conditions public schools are worth defending. The concluding sections focus on the various levels of authority, local to national, and the relationship between public and professional authority.

The Libertarian View

Perhaps the most articulate exponent of the libertarian theory, Loren Lomasky (1987), claims:

The maintenance of a liberal order is incompatible with imposed homogeneity. If a state education monopoly produces a product that is not uniformly desired by all citizens, then it quite directly impinges on their freedom to secure desired goods through voluntary exchange. . . .

In the real world it is obviously the case that no one educational package satisfies all. Views differ both as to *what* ought to be taught and *how* it should be taught. . . . Even if decisions concerning what is to be taught, by whom, and how are made entirely democratically, the result is the dispossession of minorities by the majority.

This outcome is thoroughly unjustifiable—and avoidable [emphasis in the original].[1]

Without getting into all the intricacies of his argument, let's see how Lomasky supports what is likely to appear to many to be an extreme position. According to his libertarian view, the central fact to be taken into account in developing a theory of the proper role of government is that people pursue long-term projects that give structure and purpose to their lives. These projects, says Lomasky, cover an enormous range of pursuits: "Among them are: raising one's children to be responsible adults, striving to bring about the dictatorship of the proletariat, serving God, serving Mammon, following the shifting fortunes of the New York Yankees come what may, bringing relief to starving persons in Africa, writing the Great American Novel, promoting White Supremacy, and doing philosophy."[2] Such projects provide each individual with a personal standard of value that may not and need not be shared by others.

Since personal projects differ so enormously, and since each is deemed worthwhile to its "owner," when individuals act collectively through their government, they must act in an impartial way toward all projects. It is legitimate for governments to provide goods or services, such as national defense, that would be valued by *all* project pursuers if they could not provide them for themselves, but it is not legitimate to favor some projects at the expense of others.

What is valued by all project pursuers regardless of the nature of their particular projects is the *freedom* to pursue their projects without interference from others. This freedom is a primary right that government must protect.

Although the pursuit of a personal project may sound self-centered, most people's projects include the nurture and support of others. The libertarian need not assume that people are selfish or that selfishness is a virtue. Clearly, for many parents, bringing up their own children is a cherished project, but parents have very different ideas about how this should be done and about the kinds of adults they would like their children to become. According to the libertarian, government is authorized to intervene in the home if a child's ability to become a project pursuer in his or her own right is endangered by the parents. Seat-belt laws, laws prohibiting child abuse, and the like can be justified. But beyond attempts to guarantee that children will grow up with the capacity to develop their own projects, the government must be strictly neutral with respect to the variety of ideas and approaches to child rearing and education that a diverse community maintains.

Given this kind of libertarian vision of society, it is easy to see how public schools themselves will be suspect. The public schools in a community will presumably have to make decisions about what and how to teach, decisions that satisfy the majority of taxpayers who support them. This means that parents with minority views will be coerced into contributing resources to projects they do not endorse. Take separatist groups like the Amish or the Hasidic Jews, who believe that even secular lessons must be learned in an environment suffused by religious commitment. Though they are not forced to send their children to public school, parents of Amish or Hasidic children are forced to pay taxes to those schools even when the schools follow educational programs they disdain. From a libertarian view this is a violation of freedom, both unfair and unnecessary. I argued in Chapter Two, you'll recall, that all parents ought to subscribe to my key aspirations, but the fact is that all parents don't; hence, libertarians would object to coercing people to support public schools through taxation even if they were dedicated to the three aspirations.

Challenging the Libertarian Position

In this section, designed to show the limitations as well as the surprising strength of the libertarian position, I imagine a dialogue between the libertarian and a critic.

> *Critic:* Your uncompromising defense of freedom as the mark of a good society implies complacency about present levels of inequality. Not all parents are in a position to offer a fine education to their children. Some children, lacking educational opportunities, will have a meager set of projects to choose from when they grow up, whereas children from more favored circumstances will have an enormous range. The child of corporate executives may choose to dedicate himself to his parents' enterprises or to become a beggar on the streets. To the child of the street beggar, without public schooling, commitment to building corporate empires may simply not be a viable option.
>
> *Libertarian:* I am not especially upset by the recognition that libertarian proposals permit severe inequalities, but suppose I admitted that some redistribution of resources was necessary to compensate for previous injustices. That wouldn't require me to give up my opposition to public schooling. If unequal educational resources are the problem, the rich may be taxed to provide resources to the poor, possibly in the form of educational vouchers that the poor can use to pay tuition at the private school of their choice. If evidence suggests, as it does, that poor children will learn more if they go to school in the company of middle-class children, the vouchers might, at least in theory, be worth enough to make poor children attractive to schools attended by the affluent. A strong egalitarian commitment is consistent with keeping government out of the schooling business.

Critic: Every day we read terrible stories of parents abusing or neglecting their children. Other parents may mean well but just don't know how to raise kids. We have to face the fact that many parents are not capable or fit to exercise ultimate authority over their children's education.

Libertarian: What you say may well be true, but the very same reasoning would undermine the legitimacy of policies in which these same parents participated in their capacity as democratic citizens. Of course, we recognize that a small minority of parents are not able or willing to rear children adequately, but we would argue that this is no reason to weaken parental authority in general. Since these parents would probably be a minority even in private schools, they would be unlikely to wield control in any particular school.

Critic: Let me move to an almost opposite kind of objection. Far from being indifferent to or neglectful of their offspring, many parents treat them as their own projects, bringing them up to fit a particular ideal rather than helping them to choose their own pattern of living. If the ideal libertarian society is designed to facilitate project pursuit, presumably the projects pursued should be freely chosen rather than imposed on the weaker by the more powerful. That means that there may well be a tension between children's own future projects and children *as* future projects. Libertarians may be comfortable living in a society in which promoting white supremacy is central to the lives of some of its members. But you might, or at least should, be much less comfortable with the idea that white supremacist parents have the *right* to try to make this project be central to their children as well.

Libertarian: You have a point there, and I must concede that children's vulnerability to indoctrination by their parents suggests that children's futures as autonomous project pursuers would be more secure if educational authority did not reside exclusively in their parents' hands. Even if this implication were conceded, however, that still would not autho-

rize public schooling. What it would authorize is some government regulation of private schooling. Children would
have a right at least to be exposed to a variety of projects—a
right protected by government.

Critic: Continuing my theme of potential conflict among project
pursuers, notice that adult projects may conflict as well. In
the pursuit of their project, the advocates of white
supremacy are likely to conflict with, among others, the
advocates of racial equality. Even a libertarian community
must have some means of determining in practice at what
point the pursuit of one person's or group's project infringes
on the right of another person or group to pursue its own
project. The community will have to set up some mecha-
nism to mediate such disputes, whether through courts or
legislatures or other means. In the case of conflict, members
of the community must either be prepared to plead their
own case before the authorized body or to find someone to
represent their interests. This train of thought has implica-
tions for the community's educational program. Unless all
members are taught about the community's system of conflict resolution and given rudimentary training either in representing themselves or in identifying and judging those
they designate to represent them, some members' projects
will be able to gain at the expense of others' projects. The
government's neutrality with respect to projects cannot be
maintained without a certain level of equality in the community, equality of resources *and* equality of educational
opportunity.

Libertarian: Once again, this line of criticism does suggest con-
straints on a system of private schooling, even permitting
extensive public regulation of the private education sector.
Nevertheless, it does *not* require us to abandon our opposition to government-run schools.

Critic: If you agree that projects may conflict, then you will
surely also agree that the kind of education my children

receive affects the kinds of projects you and your children can safely pursue. To take an extreme case, if I believe that the printed word is the source of all evil and keep my children from learning to read, it is much more likely that they will find themselves unemployed and you and your children will have to support them on welfare. Or if I teach them to be anarchists who respect no existing laws, they will be more likely to run afoul of the law, which will impose costs and risks on you. The good and bad consequences of children's education go well beyond the children themselves.

Libertarian: I concede your point about the "externalities" of schooling—to use economists' jargon—which does imply that the public may legitimately set educational requirements that all parents and schools must meet. Once again, however, such educational requirements needn't imply government-run schools. An analogy might be useful. Libertarians might permit governments to require infant inoculation, but they would not have to set up government clinics to do the job.

Critic: Let me offer a final challenge. Diversity may be a good thing, but there are limits beyond which it leads to anarchy. One of the founding fathers, Benjamin Rush, proposed a system of public education in 1806, arguing that "our schools of learning, by producing one general and uniform system of education, will render the mass of people more homogeneous, and thereby fit them more easily for uniform and peaceable government."[3]

Libertarian: I think your fears are exaggerated. In an age of national communications media and national labor markets, the threat of disunity is much less severe. Moreover, some degree of uniformity and quality control could be achieved through regulation and inspection, as there is with food, drugs, and airline transportation. Government schools are, I repeat, no more defensible than government airlines, government food producers, or government drug companies.

Defending Public Schooling

Many of the preceding arguments have, I hope, rebutted the libertarian insistence that the education of children be the exclusive responsibility of their own parents. A system of private schools that are publicly regulated in order to meet these challenges would probably inspire little enthusiasm among libertarians themselves. Be that as it may, libertarians would rightly note that an affirmative case for public schooling has yet to be made. Can it? It would be nice if we could directly link the three key aspirations articulated in Chapter Two to the need for public schools. Can we do that? Recall the aspirations: that students be disposed to respect evidence and that they develop the capacity and the disposition to continue their own learning. Does pursuit of these aspirations require a system of government schools? Could private schools be motivated by such aspirations? There is no reason to think that they could not. History suggests that these aspirations were pursued by some private schools long before there were public schools at all. Some might say that private schools serve these aspirations less well than public schools, but such a claim is certainly debatable.

Those who support the idea of public schooling even when they are critical of actual public schools might hope that their support for such schooling would rest on a firmer foundation than could be found in trying to extrapolate from comparative evidence about the performance of actual public and private schools. Let's review what a defender of public schooling needs to defend: a government-operated school system that (1) is democratically controlled, (2) can turn away no child, and (3) taxes the entire community to fund free education for the children who attend government schools. It is important to note here that, contrary to the rhetoric of its critics, public schools do not enjoy monopoly status and need not offer a standardized educational program to children in different schools or even in the same school.

The key distinguishing mark of public schooling is that, *in theory*, the public has the ultimate authority in determining who shall be enrolled, what shall be taught, how students and teachers shall be assigned to individual schools, and so on. Since most state constitutions guarantee all citizens the right to an education, *public schools may not exclude children because they are hard to educate*. In the private education sector, each individual school makes its own decisions about matters of curriculum, pedagogy, admissions, and the like. Private schools may refuse to admit children who are hard to educate. Parents approach private schools as they would any other private service—as consumers. In a private school, the advice of individual parents or parents as a group may be heeded but it need not be; parents can, of course, vote with their feet, but they cannot say to the principal or private school's board of directors: "This is not your school; I own a share of it. I have a *right* to be listened to."

If public schooling is to be defended, it must be partly on the basis of the role that the public (including parents, of course) has the right to play in its governance. Whatever the performance of actual schools, the idea of public schooling should be defended in part because of the opportunity it affords citizens to continue their own education by participation in policy making in an arena that is close to them geographically and emotionally. In a diverse society, many of the issues facing public schools, ranging from the abolition of tracking to the provision of contraceptives, are necessarily controversial. Because most parents feel that they have an intense stake in the success of their own children, it is hard for them to be neutral about such issues. In a private school, when an unpopular policy is adopted, parents can always pull their children out and put them in another school. In the public school context, parents who remove their children incur a higher cost, assuming that they can even find a private school that will admit them. Public school parents and other citizens have, therefore, an incentive to find a solution that is mutually acceptable to at least a stable majority of the participants. This is not only an exemplary setting for democratic problem solving but one in which participants have an incentive to respect evidence and take seriously points of view that are not their own.

A 1989 reform in the city of Chicago takes this idea seriously. The enormous school district was drastically decentralized, with ultimate educational (though not fiscal) authority residing in the hands of local school councils, each of which had to have a majority of neighborhood parents. The results of the experiment so far are mixed, but some schools show that strong democratic involvement can be a spur to meaningful reform of the educational programs themselves.[4]

The second and more important defense of public schooling depends on the fact that public schools do not choose their clients and hence typically contain a more diverse clientele than private schools. At least in theory, they embrace all children in the district, hence their original name, common schools. But why is a diverse student body an educational advantage? The answer must lie in the opportunities it provides students to confront evidence that can prompt them to enlarge their views and to confront issues and problems that can develop their motivation and capacity to learn. Let's take an example. Think of a social studies class discussing the history of relations between the western settlers and Native Americans during the nineteenth century, or the civil rights movement of the twentieth century. Imagine the character of such a discussion if the class contains African-Americans or Native American students and if it does not. The potential for a vital and passionate exchange of feelings and ideas rather than a merely academic debate is much greater in a classroom that includes descendants of the various groups involved.

Both of the points I'm making in defense of public schooling will strike defenders of private schools as debatable, to say the least. It is *private* schools, they will say, that heed parental concerns and opinions, whereas it is the more bureaucratically organized public schools that so often make parents feel unwelcome. Moreover, they will add, private school student bodies are often at least as diverse as those of public schools. Student diversity in public schools, defenders of private schools will add, far from being a resource to stimulate learning, is more likely to be a source of tension and distrust, if not outright disorder.

I do not deny these observations of actual institutions, so let me use them to clarify the point I am trying to make. The defense of public schooling depends on the ability of its defenders to show that existing schools and school systems are working to enhance the social diversity of their faculty and student bodies, to exploit that diversity for educational purposes, and to encourage citizen and especially parental involvement in policy making. Public choice and magnet school programs that attempt to overcome residential homogeneity by attracting a diverse student body to schools with distinctive educational visions appear to be moving in the right direction.

On the other hand, to the extent that citizens' rights to direct the policies of local public schools and to think of them as *their* schools is undermined by school officials and employees; to the extent that cultural, racial, and economic diversity either is discouraged or fails to be exploited to enhance students' propensity and capacity to continue learning—to that extent, those institutions deprive themselves of the only kind of justification that public schooling can legitimately offer. Consider, for example, the current experimental voucher plan in Milwaukee, Wisconsin, a plan open to no more than 1 percent of poor families in one of the most segregated school systems in the country. The opposition to even this modest effort to test the value of vouchers, an opposition led by the state school superintendent, the teachers' union, and others in the name of "public" schooling, appeared self-serving, to say the least.[5]

Schools, Libraries, and Restaurants

To get some more perspective on the question of whether public schools are justified, consider the provision of food and books in our society. Food stores and restaurants compete for customers in the private sector, and government stores and restaurants exist only in rare circumstances—in some public buildings and on military bases.

Not all people have the financial resources to feed themselves and their families, of course, but the government does not operate restaurants, much less restaurants where most of the population is expected to eat. Rather, it supplements the resources of the poor with food stamps that are redeemable at local grocery stores and supermarkets. On the other hand, consider the public's access to books and other print media. Books, newspapers, and magazines may be purchased in a variety of stores, but they may also be borrowed from public libraries. Now we can ask two questions: First, why should the government support reading at all rather than, say, woodcarving or sewing? Second, if there is something special about reading, why establish a *public* library rather than encouraging the development of private libraries and the provision of "reading stamps" to those too poor to patronize them?

I think the answer to the first question is that we believe that we should subsidize an activity, reading, that will redound to our collective benefit even if not every citizen makes use of it. But why should it matter to me whether my neighbor, whom I rarely encounter, reads anything? It should matter to me because a better-informed neighbor is likely to be a better judge of what to do about the problems that neither of us can resolve alone, problems that face us as a community, whereas it matters little to me if my neighbor is a good seamstress or woodcarver.

Can we use this reasoning to defend government-operated libraries? If individual voters have access to information bearing on the issues affecting the community, they will make better decisions and the community's business will be better taken care of. If we are to make wise collective decisions, we need access to all the facts and to unpopular as well as popular ideas; it may be adherence to the popular ideas that has gotten us into trouble. A private bookseller who stocked even a few books that were offensive to the majority might be boycotted and forced to go out of business. Public libraries, on the other hand, contain not only books and magazines that will entertain us or that will reinforce the opinions we already hold, but books and magazines that reflect dissenting, even heretical, views. They constitute a kind of public repository of ideas and images to which everyone may have access. In subsidizing reading, we collectively proclaim that evidence and argument matter, that our individual and community projects will be enhanced if we have access to a full range of ideas and information.

Libertarians might well deny the legitimacy of *both* the public library and the public school. I think a strong case can be made that public schools, like public libraries, are the natural allies of a citizenry committed to making decisions on the basis of evidence and argument. While I believe it can be argued that all taxpayers must *support* public schools, we cannot require all children to *attend* public schools, even supposing that such schools meet the criteria I mentioned earlier. The United States has always offered a home to dissenting communities, especially religious communities, who wished to turn their backs to mainstream society. So long as children's capacity to be project pursuers is not damaged, parents should not be forced to subject them to a form of schooling they deem incompatible with their deepest commitments.

The Libertarian Turns Critic

If they have followed my line of argument to this point, libertarians will passionately reject it. Since the libertarians permitted their position to be criticized, they will, rightly, expect the opportunity to reciprocate:

Libertarian: You are assuming that the entire community shares or ought to share your personal aspirations for children. The whole point of a liberal society is that it permits individuals to reach their own highly divergent conclusions about what educational aspirations to pursue. A truly liberal society, as we envision it, has no collective educational wisdom that it can require parents or schools to transmit.

My Reply: I presume that you advocate libertarianism on the basis of the powerful arguments brought on its behalf by

philosophers like Loren Lomasky. Let us suppose that
enough people agree with you and with him to bring his libertarian vision to reality. Do you wish this society now dedicated to liberal principles to be sustained over generations? I
presume the answer is yes. Do you wish succeeding generations to accept the liberal framework and respect everyone's
freedom just because it's the custom of the country or rather
because it's the best design for a good society? Again, I
assume that the question will be answered affirmatively.
Then is it not incumbent on you collectively to teach the
next generation to understand the moral basis on which
their society rests, to enable them, to the extent that their
capacity permits, to appreciate the force of the arguments
made on behalf of the libertarian point of view? Might you
not insist that all children be at least exposed to the moral
basis of their own society in whatever schools they attend,
regardless of parental wishes? Aren't you moving, then, in
the very same direction as those advocates of public schooling you so roundly condemn?

Public Schools as Symbols

The preceding discussion demonstrates that the case against public schools is not nearly as strong as hard-line libertarians would
hope, yet the philosophical case for government-operated schools
is much weaker than many of its defenders are prepared to admit.
There is one aspect of the question we have not yet considered:
What is the meaning of our having had a system of public schooling
for such a long time and what might it mean to abandon that tradition? I already alluded to this in Chapter Three. I believe that this
meaning can be discerned in the feeling expressed by many parents
who send their children to private schools, especially those who
remove their children from public schools to do so, that they are
abandoning an institution they ought to support. (I have no facts
and figures to base this on, only my own experience talking to peo-

ple over the years.)

Although most such parents are unwilling to subordinate their own children's interests as they see them in order to support their local public school, they often remove their children with reluctance. "If only the local public school were better, we'd have preferred to send Chet there," they might say. Why such reluctance to abandon an institution whose limitations they are all too familiar with? I would speculate that the answer has to do with the character of the local public school in our collective mythology, as a place where, as I mentioned in Chapter Three, children from all walks of life can learn together and benefit from each other's presence. When public schools fail, such parents feel that they have given up on the one institution that might help bridge the differences among us so that we can live together harmoniously. Although libertarians and adherents of parochial schools of all denominations might be happy to see this myth punctured, many others of us might prefer to work toward realizing rather than discarding it.

Local, State, and National Authority

Among industrial nations, the United States is distinctive in having no single, centralized educational system in which major decisions are made at the national level. Each of the fifty states possesses legal authority, but local districts traditionally have considerable autonomy. In the last decade or so, the federal government has taken an increasing interest in schooling, and a number of influential individuals and professional associations have urged greater centralization of educational efforts, including a system of national standards and national examinations in key academic subjects. For someone who argues that participation of individuals in educational policy making is one of the opportunities provided by a system of public schools, it is far from clear how to evaluate these developments.

On the one hand, the shift of the political arena from various state capitals to Washington, D.C., would put more distance between local community activists and the center of power. On the other hand, since local or statewide interest in substantive educational issues is typically slight and transitory, raising issues for debate at the national level might serve to kindle greater involvement. A basic question has not yet been addressed, however: Is there a valid reason why any educational policies need to be made beyond the local level? You may recall that in Chapter Two, I rejected the view that the primary purpose of schooling was to equip students for the labor market or even to promote democratic citizenship. Is there any educational reason why state and federal government ought even to be involved in the determination of educational policy?

It is worth noting to begin with that quite aside from recent conscious efforts to centralize decision making in education, for many practical purposes we *already* have a centralized educational system. Consider the existence of national textbook companies, national teachers' and administrators' organizations, national testing companies, elite colleges that draw students from every state, and Supreme Court decisions that constrain the autonomy of states and local districts—all of these exert a considerable standardizing influence on schooling in the United States. It is naive for advocates of local control to claim that the federal government is the primary agent of standardization. Advocates of local control over schooling might prefer to curtail rather than reinforce these centralizing tendencies, however. Schools need to educate particular children, not children in general, they might argue; therefore, those who are most familiar with those children's needs and capacities should have the most authority over their schooling.

This argument ought to carry some weight, but we should be aware of its limitations. Some matters are too important to be determined by local attitudes and mores. Should whites or blacks be able to set up "white only" or "black only" schools for their children? Should communities that take a dim view of the physically challenged be able to keep children with disabilities from attending regular public schools? Should communities that are predominantly Christian have the right to include religious instruction in the public school curriculum? Should a local community be allowed to ban a book from the school library because it was written by a Jew? I trust that most will agree that local control should not extend so far as to permit such practices.

The argument for local control also needs to be limited by an important fact. That fact is the astounding geographic mobility of the American school population. For example, between 1989 and 1990, approximately three hundred thousand children between the ages of five and nineteen, about 5 percent of this cohort, moved to a different school district, half of them to a different state.[6] Were it not for a certain level of standardization across districts and states, more students who made such a move would find themselves either repeating course content or lacking the background to follow classes at their new school.

Although efficiency in mastering content is not one of my key educational aspirations, it is obvious that children who are far ahead of or behind their peers are likely to become disaffected from further learning. What might be somewhat less obvious to advocates of local control is that, given the high rate of geographic mobility, at least a modicum of standardization is *educationally* valuable. Of course, a completely standardized curriculum limits adaptability to local conditions. The extent to which a national curriculum would either add to or reduce the number of children who were academically disaffected is, I believe, impossible to predict.

Professional Authority

So far, nothing has been mentioned about professional authority, the authority of teachers and school administrators. Professionals bridle at the notion that laypeople without expertise and experience should make decisions for them. Yet it must be recognized that in every occupation, practitioners, even those with very high levels of expertise, are guided or constrained by policies that they do not initiate.

Consider high-level foreign service officers. They pass along information and advice to their superiors in the host country and in the State Department, but they implement policies they do not originate. Sometimes those policies are set by the White House in response to public pressure by citizens with hardly any information about the situation. To take another example, military officers, even the joint chiefs of staff, who command millions of men and women, are themselves subordinate to the president, who may have little knowledge of military matters. Even physicians, although they have considerable discretion in dealing with individual patients, are constrained by laws requiring informed consent prior to performing risky procedures, permitting or outlawing certain practices, defining death, and the like. If war and diplomacy are too important to be left to the generals and professional diplomats, and health too important to be left to physicians, then education is too important to be left to teachers.

These familiar assertions cannot just be taken at face value; they need to be defended. The cases of diplomats, especially in a democracy, and physicians may appear to be very different. Diplomats are, after all, often political appointees whose job it is to serve the interests of a nation as interpreted by the secretary of state and, ultimately, the president. Diplomats are likely to know much more about a difficult situation developing in the country they're assigned to, yet it seems quite appropriate for them to implement the policies of their superiors even when those policies diverge from their own recommendations. Should physicians or other professionals defer to their clients in this manner? Philosopher Jon Moline argues that they should not, that this, indeed, is what distinguishes a profession from other occupations: "We consult them [professionals] because they profess to *know* better than we do about certain kinds of good and evil, about how to find or to avoid these."[7]

In what sense do physicians know better than we do what is good for us? Suppose that at a regular checkup I am discovered to have higher than normal (though not dangerously high) blood pressure. My physician has discovered something wrong with me that

I did not know myself. She knows, moreover, and can explain to me that if I continue to indulge my penchant for rich food and drink, the condition will worsen, putting me at risk of a heart attack. Let's imagine that, after ruminating about the matter, I decide, against the physician's advice, that I will accept the greater risk of a heart attack rather than give up a source of enormous delight. What is at issue here between the physician and myself is not whether eating rich foods is good for me—we both know it isn't—but how to weigh the risk of future serious harm, a heart attack, against the certain daily delights of a rich cuisine. Nothing in the physician's training or expertise gives her judgment special authority on this question.

When good competes with good, the professional's expertise is rightly limited. Consider the diplomacy analogy again. Looking at the situation in country X, the ambassador may know that the United States should intervene militarily. But the ambassador doesn't have to weigh the benefits of intervention against the costs to other portions of the administration's agenda. The president may conjecture that though the ambassador is right about what ought to be done in country X, military intervention will entail the sacrifice of his domestic agenda, the main reason the voters voted him into office. Whether the *total* costs of intervention are worth the anticipated benefits is a question that goes well beyond the ambassador's expertise.

Applying his notion of professional authority to teachers, Moline argues, "Teachers—especially public school teachers—are not widely trusted as professionals because many parents and others have come to believe that teachers do not know better than they what is good for their children. Some students think so, too."[8]

I think Moline need not lament this situation. Parents' understanding of their own children does often exceed that of their children's teachers. Parents have known their children their whole lives, watched them interact in many different settings, and monitored their responses to other teachers over the years. Teachers always face their students in large groups for one or at most a few hours a day for ten months. Of course, parents are unlikely to know whether their child is ready for the study of gravity and air pressure or what approach to select to introduce those topics, but they may know when it is time to relieve the pressure on their child or to raise their own expectations.

Moline says, "We trust paradigm professionals to distinguish what is truly good for us from what we perhaps childishly and unrealistically prefer."[9] Here, I agree: someone who does not think that understanding physics is a better use of children's talents than playing Nintendo should not be an educator. But does a teacher know that for Chet, learning physics is more important than learning a foreign language? Does a teacher know that a vocationally oriented program is the right thing for Esmeralda? That is far from clear.

Let's take the focus off individual children or groups of children and turn to matters of policy. Consider as illustrative a single controversial issue that surfaces from time to time: what to do about students who fall substantially behind their peers in academic performance. Should those students be retained and required to repeat a grade? Isn't this a question for the professional educational community to determine after careful study of the effects of retention? What does the evidence show? A study by Roy Doyle showed that contrary to what professionals and nonprofessionals might suppose, many lines of evidence indicate that retention neither improves the performance of those who are retained nor appreciably reduces the range of learning abilities in classrooms.[10] Although it is unlikely, suppose that the data and inferences leading to these conclusions are not challenged by other researchers. Doesn't that settle the policy issue? Is there any need or basis for nonprofessional input here? I claim there is.

Retention policies, even when they do not benefit the students who are retained, send a message to all students and parents about the seriousness of the school's expectations for a measure of academic accomplishment. In the same way that penalties for criminal misconduct may deter would-be offenders while failing to rehabilitate convicted criminals, retention policies may send a salutary signal to students and their parents about the importance of schoolwork.

Moreover, schools are supported by the public in part because progress in school is expected to bear some relation to enhanced competence. Students in the sixth grade are presumed to be able to do things that students in the third grade are not, and students who graduate from the eighth or twelfth grades are presumed to have attained some level of mastery of what is taught. Suppose that it were widely and publicly acknowledged that many students in the sixth grade actually read at a second-grade level. The effect of such an admission would be to weaken the already frail support for education that the school system needs to maintain its legitimacy. A policy of retention for academic failure provides symbolic evidence that schools are more than baby-sitting operations, evidence that is needed to maintain the credibility of the institution.

Two goods are in conflict here, public confidence in the school system and the successful educational careers of students with academic difficulties. The expertise of professionals is not sufficient to adjudicate such a conflict; it is altogether fitting that the public's elected representatives deliberate and decide the issue. It goes without saying that they would be remiss in not having the just-cited research evidence in front of them when they deliberate. Perhaps a wise school board will couple a stringent retention policy with a special program directed to students who are retained. Perhaps the board will maintain a retention policy but not monitor its enforcement too carefully.

Our society has come to appreciate that demarcating the limits of professional autonomy, even for those whom Moline designates as "paradigm professionals"—physicians, attorneys, and clergy—is a very difficult task. In disputes over educational policy, where the public holds diverse ideals of the educated person, where good almost always competes against good (and where each kind of risk must be weighed against others), it is appropriate for professional expertise to be constrained. Such disputes must be mediated through a political process in which priorities are set by the citizenry itself. This does not, of course, take away from Moline's point, which cannot be too strongly endorsed, that education itself is compromised when we lose sight of the distinction between what is good and what is merely pleasing.

Chapter Seven

Inequalities

No work hoping to reexamine fundamental educational questions can avoid the issue of inequality. This issue, however, cannot be intelligently discussed without reference to the social and economic context in which schools operate. I shall begin, therefore, by sketching out that context in a very few, necessarily crude strokes.

The Context

Let's begin with the international arena. Germany and Japan, whose military forces were no match for those of the United States and its allies in 1945, have emerged as economic powerhouses. The Soviet Union, on the other hand, only a few years ago judged by many to be a fearsome economic as well as military power, has collapsed, as has its Eastern European empire. Fierce ethnic and religious rivalries, held in check under totalitarian dictatorships, have reemerged in this part of the world and elsewhere. War or threat of war is a reality in many parts of the world. While the fear of an all-out nuclear war devastating the planet has evaporated in the space of a few years, prospects for world prosperity and stability appear just as uncertain today as they did a decade ago.

While still the world's largest economy, the United States is no longer the single dominant economic power on the world stage. Although forecasts of our economic future are probably not worth the paper they're printed on, what is certain is that the economic advantage we enjoyed in the period following the Second World War was only temporary.

During the last couple of decades, our service industries have grown but our manufacturing industries have shrunk, resulting in a substantial loss of well-paying factory jobs. Over the 1980s, while the real income of the top 20 percent of wage earners rose, the income of the remainder fell. The wages of workers with only a high school education and of younger workers fell most sharply. Between 1979 and 1991, adjusting for inflation, wages for those without a high school diploma *fell* 20 percent, wages for those with only a high school diploma fell 12 percent, wages for college graduates didn't change, and wages for those with at least two years of graduate school *rose* 8 percent.[1] As economist Lester Thurow notes, "American society is now divided into a skilled group with rising real wages and an unskilled group with falling real wages."[2]

Partly to offset losses in family income and partly in response to the opening of new opportunities and perspectives, women have joined the full-time paid labor force in growing numbers, accelerating a long-standing trend. Although two-income households have managed not to fall behind economically, single women, especially those with children, fare badly. While one out of ten married couples with children is poor, nearly half the single mothers in the United States live below the poverty line.[3]

So far as children are concerned, probably the most significant social trend affecting them is the rise in childhood poverty resulting in part from the decline in stable marriages. Writing about the effects of changing family patterns on the young, Barbara Dafoe Whitehead notes, "By 1980 only 50% could expect to spend their entire childhood in an intact family."[4] Although controversy persists about the effect on children of parents' divorce, extramarital childbearing, and remarriage, it is very hard to find evidence that these changing patterns hold benefits for children, and there is plenty of evidence to the contrary. Poverty and single-parenthood exist disproportionately among African Americans and certain other minority groups, but even among poor families headed by women, whites comprise more than half the poor and "have been the fastest growing component of this type of poverty."[5]

This extremely sketchy social inventory is somewhat misleading in downplaying the enormous racial and ethnic diversity found in our society. Our long history of racial conflict has taken a new turn in the last couple of decades. The growth of a successful and politically effective African-American middle class, due primarily to education, has contributed to the substantial increase in those living in the suburbs, albeit often segregated suburbs, of large cities.[6] At the same time, a very high proportion of African Americans remain without jobs, without homes, and without hope in inner cities and rural areas. In 1989, about half of all African-American children lived in poverty.[7] Despite several decades' efforts to desegregate public schools, the number of African Americans and Hispanic Americans attending segregated schools is *rising*. For example, close to 60 percent of the African-American children in school in the state of Illinois attend schools that have between 90 and 100 percent minority enrollment.[8]

Ever a nation of immigrants, the United States has witnessed in the last decade or so an enormous rise in the number of new immigrants, primarily from Asia and Latin America. For example, about 20 percent of the population of Los Angeles and San Francisco is foreign-born.[9] As with previous waves of immigration, many immigrant families are concentrated in certain geographic areas, many are poor, and many speak a language other than English at home. More than a hundred languages are spoken in the school system of New York City, for example.[10] Schools attended by substantial numbers of immigrant students are faced, therefore, with a considerable challenge, especially at a time in history when failure to complete high school is perceived to be a severe barrier to employment at any but the most menial jobs.

Before outlining the way the educational system responds to the situation just sketched out, let's review some basic facts. There are about forty-five million students in school between kindergarten and the twelfth grade. Of these, close to 90 percent are in public schools. Because education is not mentioned in our Constitution, ultimate educational authority resides in each of the fifty states. By historical tradition, local school districts, of which there are about fifteen thousand, enjoy considerable local autonomy, giving the United States the most decentralized educational system in the industrialized world.

In what follows I focus on resource inequalities between the favored and less favored sectors of the population because they are the most salient and least disputed. Racial and gender discrimination have, of course, traditionally existed in schools, but the extent of their persistence is debated and debatable. I briefly address the issue of gender inequality at the end of the chapter.

Many of the states with very high percentages of children living in poverty have low taxing capacities and spend much less on education than wealthier states. For example, according to the National Center for Education Statistics, in 1992, Alabama spent less than half the amount that Connecticut spent on the education of each child in the public schools.[11] Within any one state, affluent districts may spend "three or four times the amount spent on other children in the same state."[12] Hence, the differential social and economic advantages enjoyed by children of more privileged social and geographic backgrounds are reinforced by an educational system that—so far as spending is concerned— favors the more fortunate. Recent evidence substantiates what is intuitive: resources *do* make a difference to children's experiences and achievement.[13]

In concluding this section, let me note that the level of economic inequality prevalent in the United States is not found in other nations. As of 1988, the United States still enjoyed the highest per capita income in the world, but—and here the latest figures I could find are for the mid 1980s—the United States has more than 200 percent more poor people than seven major industrial nations.[14]

Can Opportunity Be Equalized?

While the facts just outlined are recognized by most students of education, there is far less agreement about how to respond to them.

Why should that be? Imagine a single fifth-grade classroom with half of the students from rich families and half from poor families and suppose that the teacher, Mr. Jones, were to spend about twice as much time with the more privileged. Wouldn't it be obvious that this was completely unfair and unjustifiable? Wouldn't the remedy be just as obvious, to spend at least equal, if not more, time with the less privileged?

Isn't the *moral* response to the social and economic inequalities recounted in the pages above just as simple? Almost, but not quite. Why not? Let's call advocates for closing the gap in educational resources the equalizers. Which arguments could challenge them? Here are three to consider. First, not all the advantaged agree that either their advantages or the plight of the disadvantaged are underserved. Some of those whose children occupy favored positions believe that they have earned their advantages for their children through hard work and sacrifice that, so they would argue, the poor have declined to emulate.

A second challenge to would-be equalizers takes the following form. The present distribution is, admittedly, unfair, yet in the long run it is better for some excellent schools to exist alongside inferior ones rather than for everyone to attend schools of equal mediocrity. The argument here would be that the scientific and technological breakthroughs needed to sustain a dynamic economy depend on having at least some children receive an outstanding education. Educational resources, these opponents of equalization might argue, are best spent on those who are most likely to benefit, those most likely to pursue advanced learning. Because of the correlation between success in school and social background, antiequalizers might argue, redistributing educational resources would harm everyone.

Third, some antiequalizers might argue that although the distribution of financial resources is unfair, a redistribution would not accomplish equalization of educational treatment, much less achievement. Simply lavishing *funds* on the children in poorer districts, it might be maintained, would not provide the kinds of parental and teacher commitment and expertise that are indispensable if academic achievement is the aim.

While there may be some merit to these arguments, at least at an abstract level, the fact that they are most often made by people who already enjoy the advantages of the present levels of unequal investment in children's futures makes them self-serving and suspect.

The real difficulty for the equalizers, however, is not moral but political. The nub of the problem is this: either any successful effort to equalize the resources available to all children must equalize *up* by raising financial expenditures in all school districts to the levels provided by the wealthiest communities, imposing a tax burden that no state could withstand, or the high spending levels in some districts must be reduced in a program to equalize *down*. Although such a policy might be favored by the less advantaged, it tends to produce defections to private schools among the affluent and, concomitantly, pressure to lower taxes from those whose children's destinies are no longer bound up to the public schools. From the standpoint of the more affluent, equalizing resources at the expense of their own children would appear to be analogous not to insisting that Mr. Jones give equal attention to all the children in his class, but to requiring him to reduce the attention he pays to the richer children in order to concentrate on the poorer ones.

The resistance by the more affluent, especially the better educated among them, to equalizing down reveals something about education that the equalizers overlook, something that makes resistance to the pressure to equalize more than the mere protection of a social advantage, though it may be just that in many instances. The point can be brought out like this: some good things that we prize are available only in a limited quantity, so that if one group has a very large share of them, another group is necessarily deprived. Homes on lakes, Model T Fords, and oil paintings by Rembrandt provide ready examples. Suppose that there are 100 lakeside homes. Once all 100 have been purchased, no one else can live in one.

Now bachelor's degrees from Princeton may be like Rembrandt paintings—not everyone can have one. Of course, we could mail everyone a Princeton diploma, but it would be worthless. Knowledge, skills, and the three key dispositions are not like that, however. Your knowing a great deal about Rembrandt's art does not limit or impede my knowing about it. On the contrary, the more people who know about Rembrandt's art, the better chance I have of learning about it. It is possible for everyone in the world to be rich in *knowledge* about Rembrandt, but it is not possible for everyone in the world to be rich in original Rembrandt paintings or in degrees from educational institutions whose reputations depend on their selectivity.

It is hard to convince affluent parents to reduce the investment they make in their children's education. Some may, as I say, be motivated only by the prospect of gaining or losing an edge in the competition for social advantage. But others, who are not focusing on social advantages and disadvantages, may rightly wonder how impoverished children across town would stand to benefit if their own children understood less, had fewer skills, or lacked the propensity to respect evidence.

Suppose that a sudden burst of economic growth were to permit the various states to equalize up. Wouldn't this create conditions under which everyone could be equally productive, resulting in a drastic reduction of income inequality? Probably not, because the favored segments of the population would still enjoy enormous advantages that the additional dollars fed into the schools of the poor could not easily buy, such as personal contacts with "movers and shakers," savvy in securing advantages for their children, safer neighborhoods, and resources to invest in after-school and summer learning opportunities. At the end of their schooling, the children of the affluent would *still* be more likely to go to college and graduate school, more likely to get good jobs, more likely to earn high incomes. All the best evidence suggests that equalizing educational treatment, even equalizing educational *achievement*, were that possible, would do little to reduce the overall disparities in income and wealth that motivated us to take such an interest in equality of educational opportunity in the first place.[15]

In a growing economy, the prospects for equalizing up are limited, but in a static or shrinking economy, they are negligible. Some states have or are contemplating strong measures to narrow the disparities between rich and poor school districts, but any redistribution that results in a perceived lowering of educational quality in more favored neighborhoods or districts is likely to be resisted now or reversed later.

A couple of episodes from neighboring small cities in my own state, Wisconsin, illustrate the difficulties of equalizing up. Two school districts, Wausau and La Crosse, devised busing plans to try to redistribute poor, low-achieving, predominantly immigrant Hmong children to all elementary schools rather than permitting concentrations of poor children in a few schools. School boards in both districts faced recall elections because of the integration plans, and in both cases incumbents favoring the income-based busing plans were soundly defeated.[16]

Dealing Fairly with Unfairness

Suppose we accept the fact that equalizing up is unlikely and equalizing down repugnant—that, in other words, once differences in educational opportunity are established, they are almost impossible to eradicate. What then? Maybe we haven't asked the right question. Let's try this one: Under what conditions would inequality of educational opportunity be acceptable to those with less opportunity? I think the answer is fairly clear: only when being in the educational winner's circle does not deprive the "losers" of the substantial benefits that society has to offer.

What makes our society so unfair to educational losers is that their access to decent-paying jobs, decent housing, health and retirement benefits, paid vacations, maternity leave, and prenatal and postnatal care for their children is reduced by their failure to earn a college degree and severely limited by failure to secure a high school diploma. A supreme irony resides in the fact that though Americans as a people are, to say the least, ambivalent about learning and intellectual achievement, so many prospects hinge on success in completing high school and, if possible, continuing on to earn a college degree. In many European countries, a much smaller proportion of students graduate from academic high schools leading to university education, but social benefits for an individual or family are much less tightly connected to academic credentials.

A decent level of well-being should not depend, as it does now, on whether one has a high school or college degree. Policies that *guarantee* to all people—regardless of the kind of job or credentials they hold—decent housing, health insurance including prenatal and postnatal care, quality preschool education, family leave to help sick children or older parents, workers' compensation, and the like, help sever the link between educational success and the basic elements of human welfare. Because some of these same guarantees help poor parents care for their young children, they also serve to reduce inequalities of opportunity to some degree. Since policies that provide assistance to young children can hardly be opposed on the grounds that children *deserve* the circumstances they are born into, such policies are also the least suspect from the moral point of view.

The kinds of policies I'm proposing will have the effect of reducing overall social inequities to some extent and possibly of reducing the incentive for students to stay in school, since the kinds of jobs available even to high school dropouts would provide more benefits—for example, health insurance—than they would otherwise have. Such policies will therefore challenge two prevalent beliefs: first, that the current level of social inequality is an economic necessity, accurately reflecting value added to society, and second, that the workforce of the future must have ever more schooling if the United States is to prosper.

Consider the first belief: I do not challenge the notion that differential compensation is needed to provide incentives for those who work harder, take more risks, have graver responsibilities, or have invested more time and money in their training. The question is whether the levels of inequality that now exist in the United States are needed to sustain a dynamic economy. Though hardly conclusive, evidence from Japan suggests that we could be as productive with reduced inequality. In 1990, Japanese chief executive officers earned 18 times as much as workers in an economy that had grown three times as fast as that of the United States. American CEOs earned *119* times as much as American workers.[17]

The notion that people are paid in direct relation to their contribution to society is hardly more credible. Consider the chief executive of Compaq Computer Corporation, who directs a workforce of ten thousand employees and received total compensation of six million dollars in 1992.[18] This gentleman earns about 40 times as much as the chancellor at my campus, who manages an organization that is double the size. Many of the highest-income earners, such as corporate officers, receive salary increases even when their companies are losing money.

The proposal to guarantee a higher level of welfare even to school dropouts seems to fly in the face of what appears to be a consensus these days about the need for a better-educated workforce. There is obviously truth to the proposition that some employees will have to work "smarter," but as has also been pointed out, many of the jobs with the largest number of anticipated vacancies are relatively low-skill jobs. For example, government forecasters anticipate that between 1990 and 2005, there will be 2,000 new jobs for mathematicians and 13,000 for chemists, compared to 587,000 new jobs for nursing and psychiatric aides and 555,000 jobs for janitors and cleaners, one of the thirty fastest-growing occupations.[19] When employers and supervisors are asked to list their sources of dissatisfaction with their employees, they are more likely to talk about poor attitudes than lack of sophisticated skills. After all, American corporations have been exporting manufacturing operations to third-world countries not because the workers there are so highly skilled, but because they have little choice other than working hard for low wages.

Many jobs, even relatively menial jobs, are performed better if employees have some ability to confront new situations intelligently and with a minimum of supervision. Here, of course, it is the capacity and disposition to keep on learning that really count, not mastery of particular skills or facts. Employers do complain that high school graduates can't perform simple arithmetic operations or write a grammatically correct application letter, and a number have found it necessary to institute their own programs in basic education. But, I believe, the conventional diagnosis of the problem is deeply flawed.

This diagnosis points to an insufficient number of hours in school, low-quality teaching or textbooks, insufficient homework, and the like. Consider Jeff, a representative student in the bottom quarter of his tenth-grade class with no diagnosed cognitive impairment. Is it plausible that 2,000 hours of instruction were not sufficient for Jeff to learn to solve a fairly easy arithmetic problem, even allowing for mediocre teaching and textbooks? Is it plausible that 2,400 hours of instruction in English and language arts were not enough for Jeff to learn to write a simple business letter? Would longer school days, shorter vacations, more homework, or fewer pupils per teacher have made the difference? This just isn't plausible.

Two hypotheses appear much more plausible to me: (1) that Jeff's disposition or capacity to learn was damaged before he entered school (or even during his early schooling) or (2) that Jeff's prospects for success relative to his highly ranked peers may appear so bleak that he sees no point in trying to learn what his teachers intend him to. Indeed, Jeff is far more likely to become part of an oppositional culture whose efforts are focused on resisting the invitation to academic learning with all his considerable energy. Perhaps Jeff will comply to a minimal degree in order to get his diploma, or perhaps he will drop out; in neither case will academic learning have any attraction for him.

The conservative response to Jeff is that the school's regime is too lax, the standards are too low, and he cannot be expected to graduate unless he performs at a much higher academic level. I challenge that response. Added pressure to perform may indeed raise Jeff's performance level somewhat—though it may also hasten his exit from school— but I don't think that it will enhance his capacity or rekindle his disposition to learn very much.

We must confront the possibility that Jeff's capacity and disposition to learn might be enhanced if he were to spend *less* time in conventional academic classrooms. This kind of thinking appears dangerous to some egalitarians who worry about the social consequences of a faltering commitment to the academic education of all children through twelfth grade. But why only through twelfth grade? Isn't a diploma from a four-year college the credential needed for access to the "good jobs"? Would even that be sufficient? A recent *New York Times* article notes that the recent cuts in middle-management jobs have resulted in college graduates taking blue-collar jobs formerly reserved for high school graduates.[20] We could insist that everyone earn a liberal arts college degree, but probably even the most dedicated exponent of universal liberal education would realize that mandating four years' attendance at a liberal arts college would not really benefit those who already find high school attendance a waste of their time. But are twelve years in conventional academic classrooms of undoubted benefit to all students? Surely the answer is not an obvious yes.

I believe that the egalitarians just referred to, now joined with many neoconservatives in their call for a rigorous academic education for all students, share what psychologist Mihaly Csikszentmihalyi calls "continued allegiance to an impossible ideal of mass salvation through liberal education."[21] Is there a way of backing away from this "impossible ideal" without exacerbating the class and ethnic divisions that already exist? *That* is the critical question.

Part of the answer lies in the direction I have already laid out, in decoupling access to a decent life from performance in school. No more than race or creed should educational attainment or achievement be a basis for granting or denying a person the resources needed to live and bring up children with dignity.

Another part of the answer lies in increasing public provision of diverse educational opportunities throughout the life span. Still another part of the answer, I believe, lies in experimenting with a broader range of educational programs to meet the diverse interests and capabilities of young people. Here I do not refer to teaching the same material at different levels or to echoing current rhetoric urging pedagogical accommodation to diverse "learning styles." Rather, by keeping in mind the fundamental aspiration of developing the disposition and capacity to keep learning throughout life, we can legitimately experiment with many kinds of experiences. Let me give one example. For the more affluent, travel abroad has traditionally been the capstone of a complete education. Even Jean-Jacques Rousseau recommended travel as essential to a student's development. Might various kinds of guided travel experiences stimulate a desire to learn on the part of students like Jeff? We've never really thought about it.

It's strange that while on the one hand we hear a clarion call to celebrate diversity, on the other, we still search for the one best system of educating everyone, to use historian David Tyack's phrase. It's unfortunate that while a large number of very exciting educational experiments are under way in both public and private schools, many of them eliciting loyalty and enthusiasm from teachers and students, most of these experiments will be abandoned within a few years because they do not raise achievement test scores. And it's unfortunate that some of the most exciting learning opportunities—summer music, drama, and science programs; backpacking trips in the wilderness; and programs for the gifted and talented such as Future Problem Solving—are rarely open to Jeff and his peers in the bottom quartile. While Jeff's more favored peers are participating in such programs, Jeff is expected to develop his intellect by filling out more commercial worksheets, watching more educational films, and taking more quizzes. Surely, Csikszentmihalyi is right that for the likes of Jeff, "much of the learning in schools is neither useful nor enjoyable; rather, it has the character of an empty ritual whose meaning has been forgotten."[22]

Grouping Students

What I've just proposed appears to lead directly to tracking and to vocational education. Did I not say at the outset that training workers was a contemptible aspiration for an educational system? Am I retreating from that judgment? Let me repeat once again the fundamental commitment enunciated at the outset: the key aspirations are that all students shall maintain a disposition and a capacity to learn, and that they shall care about evidence relevant to the conclusions they draw. What I am trying to dislodge is the notion that a one-size-fits-all program of studies is the appropriate vehicle for pursuing those aspirations, given the enormous diversity of American students. It's conceivable to me that Jeff, at age fifteen, after reviewing the evidence of his past academic accomplishments and present proclivities, and *with my key aspirations in mind*, would opt for an apprenticeship program, or decide to pursue evening studies while holding down a job, or choose to work for a year or two and then decide whether to pursue a high school diploma. It's also quite conceivable to me that his parents and school counselor would concur in that decision. Must we, who have placed respect for evidence so high on our list of aspirations, conclude that Jeff is necessarily mistaken?

Not many generations ago, a girl who lost her virginity before marriage was considered "fallen," unfit for wedded life. Today's high school dropout is a contemporary equivalent, a fallen person. We no longer believe that loss of virginity prior to marriage dooms a woman. Must we continue to believe and act as if a person who drops out of school before graduating forfeits all hope of a satisfying life?

Maybe I seem to be avoiding rather than confronting the issues of tracking and ability grouping. Tracking, the separation of cohorts in high school according to their probable paths after graduation, is usually distinguished from ability grouping, the grouping together of students of like levels of educability for ease of instruction. In theory, it is easy to distinguish the two ideas, but in practice it is hard for ability grouping not to become de facto tracking, especially if it is employed consistently throughout students' schooling. Both tracking and ability grouping appear natural, even inevitable, to some, yet anathema to others. Why? As in so many perennial disputes, each side has at least one legitimate point that the other overlooks.

Proponents are right in believing that not all students can profit from the same instruction. The same lesson may be perceived by some children as moving much too slowly, while others are struggling to keep up. Cooperative learning programs may mute some of these differences, but eventually, unless the entire credential system is dismantled, either the swift or the slow learners will feel cheated. Of course, a girl who's quick at mathematics may not be quick at music or basketball, though some children excel in everything they do and, regrettably, others find it hard to do anything well. To deny in the academic realm what appears incontrovertible in every other part of life seems to me to show scant respect for the evidence.

Opponents of tracking or other forms of ability grouping also have a hold on some undeniable facts. Tracking does perpetuate social and racial advantages and disadvantages. In schools with different tracks, the students from the less privileged and less white parts of town are likely to be concentrated in the tracks leading straight to full-time employment or to two-year colleges at best. Opponents of tracking correctly believe that far from receiving the best education that could be designed for them, the students in the low tracks often receive an inferior education from every standpoint, certainly from my own. The purported pedagogical advantages offered to all by tracking, in theory, are, in fact, bestowed on those in the high tracks.

The extent to which the ability to master academic subject matter is inborn, the extent to which it results from early experiences at home, and the extent to which it is an artifact of schooling itself are questions of continuing controversy that are not likely to be settled soon. Moreover, the extent to which "deficits" can be reversed through intensive intervention in the preschool years or in school is not known either, because we have never invested in the future of a group of poor children extravagantly enough and for a long enough time to find out; nor are we likely to. It does seem apparent, however, judging by the efforts we *have* been willing to make so far to help the poorest children get ready for school, through programs such as Project Head Start, that these efforts have not yielded remarkable academic accomplishments a decade or so later.

Current leaders of the educational reform movement appear to me to be well aware, and properly so, of the evils of tracking, but they tend to turn their backs on the causes of differential educability. Neoconservative Chester Finn does so, for example, by simply proclaiming, "Whether limited or comprehensive, the core of what is learned must be the same for all Americans. Never again should curricular tracking darken our doors."[23] Marshall Smith, undersecretary of education under President Bill Clinton, and Jennifer O'Day almost echo Finn when they argue for a "common content core" in which "all students must be *expected* and *given the opportunity* to perform at the same high standards on a common assessment."[24]

It is easy to utter or type the words "common challenging content," "eliminate tracking," and the like, which sound suitably egalitarian. Ask yourself, though: Will a nation like ours, with at least a streak of contempt for book learning and bookish people, a nation loathe to invest in those not yet old enough to vote, a nation that embraces the proverb "Those who can, do; those who can't, teach"—will such a nation, in a time of severe fiscal austerity, succeed in creating schools in which *all* children learn "challenging content"? I just can't believe it.

Let's go back to the reasons why the present tracking system is so unworthy of our acceptance: it does not succeed educationally by anyone's standards, least of all my own, and it reinforces invidious social distinctions between groups. Now it is quite possible to imagine an educational system that would no longer have official tracks with designations like "college prep" and "vocational."

Indeed, an official system of tracks is neither necessary nor desirable, but it will be difficult for high schools, especially those that cater to a large and heterogeneous student body, to avoid grouping students by educability—that is, by preparation for mastering academic subjects at different levels of sophistication. A school that determined to eliminate all ability grouping would be vulnerable to abandonment by academically capable children of affluent parents, who would opt for private schooling. Just because of the correlation between educability and social background, ability grouping will, in effect, create a tracking system, whether it is so labeled or not.

The only fair solution is the one I have proposed: the link between school success and subsequent social benefits and opportunities must be *loosened*, not tightened as so many are advocating.

The idea of a common core for all students is often seen, not only as a remedy for inequality of opportunity, but also as a way to provide a unifying foundation for an extremely diverse society. Finn claims that "universal mastery of a common core is what will hold us together as Americans."[25] I have already taken issue with the notion that education is to be equated with familiarity with some particular set of references or works, but aren't the fears of disunity real, and doesn't a common curriculum have something to offer in this regard?

I don't know if there is a greater threat of disunity today than there was in the past, but if there is, I'm quite sure that it doesn't come from the absence of a common fund of information. After all, everybody knows who Bill Cosby and Madonna are, if not who Hawthorne and Emily Dickinson were. Remember, it's what people are disposed to do and what they care about that ultimately matter. The fear of fragmentation is, at bottom, a fear that not everyone cares about the same things. Take an example: a recent film, *Menace II Society*, depicts a segment of African-American society in which adolescent gang members murder their rivals or even innocent people with little provocation and no apparent remorse. The portrayal is shocking and frightening, not least because it shows how far we are from sharing a "common core" that holds us together. The distance that separates the reader of this book from an adolescent gang member who kills to earn respect has little to do, however, with the official syllabi or textbooks used in our public schools. In fact, since a national market for textbooks exists that is dominated by a few companies, I would not be surprised to learn that the reader's children have been exposed to the very same textbooks as the gang members.

It may be true that no nation can exist without some common reference points that would be understood by everyone. My guess is that worries about the absence of such common reference points are probably less well founded today than at any time in our history. A passage from an essay by the novelist Wallace Stegner about the American West sums this up nicely: "But is anything except their setting distinctive? The people . . . eat the same Wheaties and Wonder Bread and Big Macs, watch the same ball games and soaps and sitcoms on TV, work at the same industrial or service jobs, suffer from the same domestic crises and industrial blights, join the same health clubs and neighborhood protective associations, and in general behave and misbehave much as they would in Omaha or Chicago or East Orange. The homogenizing media have certainly been at work on them, perhaps with more effect than the arid spaciousness of the region itself."[26]

As I pointed out in Chapter Five, we already have many elements of a national curriculum, not just the general cultural curriculum Stegner identifies, but the curriculum provided by national subject matter and teachers' organizations, national testing companies, federal mandates and programs, and the national textbook industry. Don't misunderstand me: there *is* a problem about whether our nation can hold together and prosper in the coming decades, one that I have no wish to minimize. Insofar as teachers model and call attention to what the younger generation ought to care about, they have a role in the resolution of that problem. As I see it, the question of whether we (and the next generation) have a common core—not merely a common fund of information, but one that will genuinely hold us together—is not a question that teachers can be expected to answer. It is either naive or disingenuous for us to pretend the contrary.

Gender Inequality

Just because, historically, women's status and power depended on those of their husbands or fathers—in some cases very high, in others, very low—their situation can't be compared to that of African Americans or Native Americans. A veritable revolution in the status of women has occurred in the last generation, but gender inequalities persist. Women have not only entered new fields but become prominent in professions ranging from accounting to zoology, yet they often fail to attain the very highest levels of decision-making authority. In some fields—engineering, finance, and surgery, for example—the proportion of women participants is still very low. As with the other inequalities I've discussed, opinions differ about the extent to which lingering inequalities are the result of discriminatory treatment, free choices made by women themselves, ostensibly neutral but gender-biased definitions and norms of success, or biologically rooted differences.

Curricula and classroom practices have been held partially responsible for lingering inequalities. Obvious and subtle differential treatment of boys and girls in schools has been brought to the attention of teachers and textbook writers. Patterns of differential treatment have been gradually changing as women have been encouraged to pursue avenues once reserved for males only (but not vice versa).

Throughout this period of changing gender relations, the underlying thrust has been to eliminate differential gender treatment in order to equalize opportunity for women. The relative success of many of these efforts has also served to highlight areas that are resistant to this strategy. Two somewhat different educational approaches to these more intractable inequalities may be identified: (1) the resegregation of women from men has been advocated in some quarters and (2) some feminists have attempted to challenge the notion that male-oriented occupations and styles of behavior should constitute the norm for women to emulate. Let me say a brief word about each.

There appears to be some validity to the idea that women's intellectual development may be fostered in all-female settings. Girls' math skills, for example, usually lag behind boys' and some public schools have been experimenting with female-only math classes.[27] I think it highly unlikely, however, that such settings will proliferate. Segregation of boys and girls is not logically incompatible with the goal of adult gender equality, but I think it would seem so to most parents. If the goal is for women to interact with men as equals, it would seem incongruous to prepare them for that state of affairs by limiting their associations with males during the formative years.

The attempt to depreciate male styles and norms also has a certain plausibility. Consider a concrete example. It is expected in certain traditionally male-dominated professional fields—mainstream scientific research or corporate law, for example—that people will work sixty hours a week or more; men with such schedules have "naturally" relegated homemaking responsibilities to their wives. When women first entered these demanding occupations, they often had to (or wanted to) show that they could work just as long hours as men. Now some women wish to challenge the equation of long hours with success. They would like to redefine success to include caring for a household and children, responsibilities that ought to be shared by both spouses. They want to ensure that men as well as women share in the tasks of nurturing the next generation and hence that schools avoid making outdated assumptions about women's (and men's activities). I certainly support these efforts.

This sensible argument is taken a step further by some radical feminists: pursuits such as corporate law or scientific research, they argue, are themselves fundamentally male pursuits—unhealthy, destructive—and unworthy of women's commitment. I find this kind of argument both dubious and politically dangerous for the cause of women's equality. Feminists who argue that the very enterprises of science or law are organized around male values are only echoing generations of sexist males who insisted that women were not equipped for careers in science or law. Such arguments do nothing to challenge male dominance in prestigious fields, while they cast doubt on the femininity of women who succeed in them. The gap between men's and women's educational achievements is continually being narrowed, where it exists at all. This is hardly the time for feminists to try to devalue the pursuits that generate the most power and prestige in our society.

Chapter Eight

Change

We are told that the world is changing fast, perhaps too fast for us to grasp, much less adapt to, yet according to almost every book or article on the subject of education, schools are not changing nearly fast enough.

Have schools changed at all, and if so, how? Should we support the chorus of calls for dramatic changes in schooling? What are the barriers to change? How should we think about school reform? These are the questions I'll deal with in this chapter.

Have Schools Changed?

There are different views on whether schools have changed over the last seventy-five years or so since compulsory primary and secondary schooling became a reality in this country. One view, which we might call the pendulum theory, suggests that changes in schooling are like pendulum swings—changes made in one epoch are repudiated in the next and then reintroduced again as a new cycle begins. In this view, change is constant; the pendulum is always going back and forth, yet it never leaves its place. Let me label the second view the cockroach theory, after that hardy creature known to have survived through eons of time through its ability to adapt to virtually any environment. According to this view, schools are always and everywhere the same. Finally, consider what could be called the coral reef theory. Here, the idea is that schools do change and the changes trace a perceptible pattern, but the changes are so slow and gradual that they are not evident from year to year. Which, if any, of these theories have merit?

I think pendulum-like cycles are discernible. Sometimes these cycles are the result of the changing focus of public concern. There are, for example, observable cycles in which the public focuses on the needs of different segments of the student population. After a period during which "life adjustment education" was perceived to be the dominant educational ideology, reformers of the 1960s urged a refocus of attention to the academic mission of the school, emphasizing the need to train a scientific elite to meet the perceived threat posed by Soviet technological advances. In less than a decade, public concern shifted to the plight of the "disadvantaged" and a concern with equity replaced the focus on training the elite for leadership. The early eighties heard a renewed call for holding students to "world-class" standards in science and mathematics. Now the "excellence" movement has been muted a bit and there is concern that students should not be judged against standards they have not had the opportunity to work toward.

Other pendulum-like patterns are discernible as well. Schools and school districts were once quite small, especially in rural areas. In the middle of the twentieth century, the movement to consolidate small districts and build larger schools to benefit from economies of scale gathered strength. Very recently, recognition that huge schools and school districts carry some serious disadvantages has created a trend toward smaller school districts and smaller schools—the latter sometimes achieved through the establishment of a number of separate schools within large school buildings. Similar swings may be detected regarding attitudes toward students whose academic progress is unsatisfactory. After a period in which prevailing sentiment held that such students should not be advanced to the next grade, a period during which retention in grade lost favor was to be expected—only to be followed, again, by a reaction in favor of more stringent standards for promotion.

Such pendulum-like patterns are sometimes thought to be the result of faddishness among educators, but they derive, I think, from a more basic feature of schools, one to which I'll return below, namely that some of the legitimate aspirations of teachers or parents can only be achieved at the expense of others. A small school, for example, offers a more homelike atmosphere; on the other hand, a small school cannot afford the facilities (state-of-the-art science laboratories, for example) needed for certain educational possibilities to be realized. When one value is being consistently sacrificed to another, it is likely that constituencies with an interest in the value that's out of favor will mobilize in order to restore "balance"; it is highly probable that the resulting "correction" will eventually appear to opponents to have gone too far in the other direction.

The cockroach theory is most apt when applied to the micro-level, the process of teaching and learning within classrooms. A thought experiment gives it some credibility: imagine your great-great-grandparents brought back to life and plunked down in a second-grade classroom in the midst of a reading lesson or in a high school classroom where a lesson in geometry is taking place. Would they have any difficulty in understanding what was going on? It is unlikely that they would. Most classrooms, past and present, whether in this or any other country, do contain similarities. A single teacher almost always faces a group of students, at least some of whom would rather be doing other things than learning the lesson the teacher has planned. The threat of disorder, of children running around, talking out of turn, whispering to neighbors, or disrupting the lesson with jokes or pranks is present in almost every classroom and evokes familiar stratagems in response: rules and routines, examinations, threats, attempts to win over or intimidate instigators, and raised voices of admonition. Books, notebooks, pencils or pens, and chalkboards are the tools that teachers and students have used for decades. Typically, teachers expound, explain, demonstrate, ask questions, correct answers. Typically, the subjects taught include, first and foremost, reading and writing in the national language, the rudiments of mathematics, some science and history, some art, music, and physical education.

Last year I watched an episode of the popular television cartoon, *The Simpsons*, in which Bart Simpson and his elementary school teacher, a middle-aged woman with no sense of humor, engaged in the kind of duel that would strike a chord of recognition in fourth graders, their parents, or their grandparents. What causes this stability? Part of the answer lies, I believe, precisely in the challenge a sizable group of young people poses to a single adult charged with keeping order in a classroom, a challenge that conventional pedagogy answers. Part of the answer lies simply in the absence of the ingredients necessary for dramatic change, a topic to which I'll return below.

The cockroach theory is not the whole story, however. Over the last century or so there have been changes in schooling of the kind that fit the third theory, the coral reef theory. According to this theory, gradual changes do occur, changes that are barely visible in the short run but that cumulatively are highly significant.[1] Let me mention nine of the most prominent:

1. Schooling has expanded to occupy more years and more hours of the day.

2. Access to schooling for women and nonwhite minorities has increased.

3. There has been a growing informality and friendliness between teacher and student, with less overt shaming or corporal punishment. Informal dress, speech, and demeanor are apparent. Students, especially younger students, move about the classroom more easily and whisper or talk to neighbors from time to time without expecting to be reprimanded. The movable furniture that has replaced rows of bolted-down desks in most classrooms reflects this gradual trend away from regimentation and formality in student-teacher relations.

4. Schools themselves, especially middle and high schools, have tended to expand to include larger numbers of students. Partly for this reason, classrooms are much less likely to include children of diverse ages as was common in smaller and, of course, one-room schools. Not only do many more children occupy a single school building, but there has been a proliferation of professional roles: guidance counselors, social workers, psychologists, remedial reading specialists, specialists in the education of children with disabil-

ities, assistant principals, teachers' aides, and so on. In place of a group of teachers under a single "principal" teacher, we now often find a sizable, hierarchical organization.

5. The last seventy-five years have seen a proliferation of extracurricular activities of all kinds, but especially athletics. After the end of the official school day but still under the school's auspices, students can pursue interests in chess, wrestling, or band, to name just three of perhaps dozens of activities that are featured in a large high school. Especially in small towns and rural areas, the fortunes of the football team may be much more important to the life and morale of the community than the rise and fall of SAT scores.

6. There has been a trend toward greater differentiation of courses and entire programs geared to different portions of the student body, especially in high schools. The availability of vocational programs is especially noteworthy. Training for occupations ranging from auto repair to data analysis to child care coexists under the same roof with academic programs. Electives and alternative courses or tracks have replaced uniform academic courses for all students at a particular grade level. Over time, the school itself has taken a more active role in sorting out children for various kinds of programs connected to different "probable destinations."

7. Over time, many courses have adopted a more functional (as opposed to cultural) focus. For example, math classes are more likely to deal with problems associated with being a consumer, buying on credit, and the like. Social studies classes focusing on the rights and responsibilities of citizenship have been added to an earlier era's devotion to history. English classes are more likely to teach such skills as writing a business letter instead of focusing exclusively on literature and grammar.

8. The growth in the size and complexity of individual schools has been accompanied by a growth in the size and complexity of an educational bureaucracy and a long-term trend toward centralization.

9. Preparation for teaching has become much more extensive and teachers have organized themselves into unions or professional

organizations to represent their interests. Once barely earning a living wage and subject to arbitrary dismissal or transfer by administrators, teachers now have strong organizations to back them in wage disputes and to protect them against disciplinary action or dismissal without just cause. In fact, once a teacher earns tenure, normally after three years of satisfactory performance, suspension or dismissal is extremely difficult and very rare.

Sources of Social Change

It could be said, I think, that many of these gradual developments represent the efforts of schools to adapt to the fact that for an unprecedented proportion of the eligible population, virtually *all* those between the ages of six and eighteen, daily attendance at school is the mandatory path to membership in adult society. Some would say that the cumulative impact of these gradual changes is profound. In any case, the cockroach metaphor is far from apt to describe them.

Despite coral reef changes, I think it is still fair to say that the core activities of teaching and learning in school classrooms have not been transformed dramatically. Should we have expected them to? There is a tendency to see pedagogical stability as a sign of the backwardness of the educational sector or of its resistance to innovation.

A characteristic response to pedagogical stability comes from Massachusetts Institute of Technology professor Seymour Papert, a pioneer in the design of computer software for education. Papert poses this question in his recent book, *The Children's Machine:* "In the wake of the startling growth of science and technology in our recent past, some areas of human activity have undergone megachange. Telecommunications, entertainment, and transportation, as well as medicine, are among them. School is a notable example of an area that has not. . . . Why, through a period when so much human activity has been revolutionized, have we not seen comparable change in the way we help our children learn?"[2]

It is almost expected that influential leaders and certainly critics will issue calls not just to extend or modify coral reef trends, but to initiate dramatic changes, or megachanges, in the way the core activities of teaching and learning are carried out. Are such megachanges a real possibility? To help us think about this, let's look at a couple of examples of dramatic change. Consider doing the laundry as an everyday activity that has evolved dramatically since the turn of the century; if our great-great-grandparents were reincarnated, they would marvel at the way this activity is carried out today. At the turn of the century, a family's wash would take at least half a day, longer if we take into account the time needed for clothes to dry outdoors and the time needed subsequently for folding and ironing. Today, not only is the washing and drying done by machine, but many garments come out of the drier ready to wear. The actual labor needed to do the job may be measured in minutes, with folding and putting away the clothes constituting the most time-consuming part of the task.

This change in laundry habits did not happen all at once. Even such dramatic changes evolve more gradually than we realize. The invention of a way to bring well water into the house and of laundry soap; the subsequent invention of primitive manual washers and wringers, leading to the invention of increasingly sophisticated washers and driers that run on gas or electricity; the invention and continual improvement of synthetic fabrics that don't require ironing—these developments began about one hundred fifty years ago and are still continuing.[3]

The development of new laundry technology is just a small part of the story of the transformation of household labor over the past century, a story that includes the invention of the refrigerator and freezer, gas and electric stoves, microwave ovens, and frozen and prepared food, to name but a few of the most obvious innovations. The transformation of patterns of living in the household and the changing role of women in society from domestic workers to part-time or full-time wage earners outside the home would have been impossible without these technological developments. This is not to say that the inventions came first and the social transformation followed as simple cause and effect. Change doesn't work only in a single direction. After all, the invention of new technologies does-n't change lives unless those technologies are actually employed, which requires them to be successfully marketed. This means that those who pay the bills must feel that they are getting value for their money; for example, they may believe that the new technologies will enhance the family's status if not actually improve the quality of their lives. The cause-and-effect relationships involved in such social transformations are enormously complex, and it would require a trained historian to begin to sort them out. Still, an informed analysis could not deny the general point illustrated by my exam-ple: technological change is a powerful catalyst for dramatic social change.

Some dramatic social changes do occur, however, without any obvious technological underpinning. Think, for example, of the changed status of African Americans in the South resulting from the civil rights movement. Within a couple of decades after Rosa Parks refused to give her seat to a white man on a bus in Mont-gomery, Alabama, in 1955, the legally required separation of blacks and whites in public places was over—which does not mean, of course, that either an integrated or a fully equal society emerged. Still, blacks could be found in many places from which they had previously been barred, including state legislatures. If Rosa Parks's grandparents had been reincarnated in 1975, they would have been astounded at the advances made by African Americans in claim-ing their rightful place as equals. Here, too, let us remember that the struggle for civil rights for African Americans did not begin in 1955. Although events happened swiftly in the period from 1955 until the passage of the Civil Rights Act of 1964, the groundwork for dramatic change had been prepared over decades.

What made it possible for African Americans, separated from and subordinated to whites in the South for two centuries, to suc-cessfully assert their rights to equal citizenship in the decade fol-lowing Rosa Parks's arrest? The story is, of course, a complex one, but any adequate account would include, at a minimum, the following elements: the success of black leaders in organizing massive nonviolent resistance; the economic threat to the white Southern power structure posed by boycotts and the threat of boycotts; the fear of increasing armed violence and chaos if concessions were not made; the mobilization of liberal whites in the North; the living example of the North, a more prosperous region in which African Americans didn't labor under the legal disabilities they suffered in the South; and, finally, the increasing difficulty that whites faced —a difficulty brought home through a new technology of communication, television—in trying to reconcile mistreatment of blacks with the egalitarian sentiments expressed in the nation's founding documents.[4]

From these examples, we might infer that future dramatic changes in the core processes of teaching and learning would depend either on the evolution of powerful new technologies that transformed the nature of teaching and learning or on the ability of one group of participants (perhaps parents or teachers or children) to mobilize a mass movement in favor of pedagogical change. Other catalysts for dramatic change may appear, for example, catastrophes such as war or economic collapse, but if they did have a direct effect on the core activities of teaching and learning, it is very likely that the society would seek to reverse that impact once the calamitous period ended.

Prospects for Dramatic Changes in Teaching and Learning

We may focus our discussion of the prospects for megachange in teaching and learning on technology and mass social movements. Because the second possibility has limited plausibility, it needn't detain us for very long. Children and adolescents obviously don't have the ability to organize themselves beyond a single school to lead a mass movement. Disgruntled parents do have that ability. Parents have mobilized to change schooling, but agitation by parents is not likely to be aimed at the core activities in the classroom. Disgruntled parents are likely to be either those whose children are not succeeding in school or those whose children are currently successful but who feel that success to be jeopardized. Judging by past experience, we could imagine parents mobilizing for a variety of educational reforms—desegregation, school safety, parental choice, smaller class size, and the like—but it's difficult to imagine parents mobilizing for a transformed pedagogy. Why?

As the civil rights movement illustrates, mass mobilization is most likely when one segment of the population feels deprived of rights or privileges that are accorded to the majority. Insofar as we can imagine parents mobilizing for a more effective pedagogy, it would no doubt be for the kind of pedagogy enjoyed by the more favored segments of the population. Since that pedagogy is, with rare exceptions, more traditional than revolutionary, it is difficult to imagine a mass, parent-led movement agitating on behalf of pedagogical transformation.

What about teachers? Could we imagine a teacher-led mass movement for a transformed pedagogy? That, too, is difficult. Teachers have been socialized in conventional classrooms. Most of their teacher training courses have employed conventional pedagogy. They have internalized the traditional expectations, reinforced by administrators, by parents, and by students themselves. Teachers can become enormously frustrated by their work life, but they are likely to act on that frustration either individually by leaving the occupation or collectively by demanding changes such as higher pay, greater autonomy, and more preparation periods. In other words, it's easy to imagine teachers demanding greater societal rewards and recognition for the job they have been assigned, hard to imagine them agitating to change the nature of the work itself. Is transformation of learning through new technologies more likely?

Papert claims, "With much more persuasive power than the philosophy of even so radical a thinker as Dewey, the computer, in all its various manifestations, is offering the Yearners [those who yearn for something different] new opportunities to craft alternatives."[5]

Computers are only the latest in a line of technological innovations that include television and film, innovations that hold out hope to those who see technology as the key to transforming activities in school classrooms.

Just as early films resembled traditional plays staged in front of a camera instead of a live audience, so, Papert would be the first to agree, much computer software is modeled on the pedagogy of conventional teachers delivering standard packages of information to students in the form of questions, answers, and drills. Sometimes the skills or information to be learned are embedded in games and puzzles that motivate students, and many such programs are sufficiently engaging to hold the students' interest for a considerable time. This use of computers permits children with different learning profiles and interests to work on different topics or different levels of the same topic simultaneously without creating undue logistical difficulties for the teacher. Such programs, though they reinforce conventional ideas about learning, could still help transform the nature of *teaching* by freeing up teachers to attend more closely to other tasks, such as helping students deal with emotional or social problems or leading small-group discussions.[6]

Papert has a different and radical vision of learning with computers, albeit one that depends for its inspiration on the progressive tradition that stretches back to Rousseau. Let's consider a couple of learning experiences he describes in his new book. One is a collaboration between two fifth-graders, Brian, a dancer, and Henry, a math whiz, who together designed a computer animation displaying "dancing" shapes. Papert notes of these students:

They certainly mastered a great deal of technical mathematics. Moving those objects on the screen required a description of the movements in mathematical language that went beyond even Henry's previous knowledge. They represented an object's speed as a variable, and then set up formulas to vary it. They learned to think of directions as angles measured in degrees. They picked up the idea of doing geometry by coordinates in a way much closer to the living and personal discovery through which René Descartes first came upon it than to the deadly formal presentation of math textbooks. But this kind of knowledge was only a small part of what they learned.

Beyond developing technical mathematical skills, they came to experience mathematics in a very different way. It became something to be used purposefully; they felt it as a source of power in pursuing important and deeply personal projects.[7]

In another chapter, Papert describes a fourth-grade Lego-Logo workshop, which provided an ample supply of Lego plastic building bricks, gears, motors, sensors, and computers that could be connected to the motors and sensors.[8] Children were allowed to design and build their own devices, individually or in small groups. Many of the boys built trucks or robots that could be operated from a computer or that contained sensors that responded automatically to their environment. Papert describes in considerable detail the progress of Maria and a small group of girls who concentrated on building a Lego house but initially shunned involvement with the technology. He describes their decision to try to install a blinking light in the house and the trial-and-error way they finally figured out how to program the computer so that the light would blink as they wished it to.

What is the teacher's role in such a project? Papert rejects the idea that the teacher should have assigned the project to the group or designed a computer program that could have helped diagnose the problems the students were having in order to facilitate more efficient learning. That way of thinking, he claims, "risks missing an essential fact":[9]

What was empowering for Maria and her friends was not making the lights blink but finding their own way to get around their own internalized obstacles. Although a teacher might, of course, have given some guidance in this, it is hard to imagine a more delicate teaching task or one that I would be less inclined to entrust to any contemporary computer's power to make decisions. As a teacher I would see my best contribution as reviewing the story afterward in a way that would consolidate the students' awareness of how well they had done.[10]

The vision of education described in these scenarios is dramatically different from the vision that informs the conventional classroom, even at its best, as in Jim Minstrell's physics classroom described in Chapter Three. While Minstrell does not see his role as that of a transmitter of information, he does have a clear pedagogical goal and an agenda for reaching it. In Papert's vignettes, the children formulate their own goals for themselves and depend on their own and their classmates' resources for reaching them. Of course, the materials themselves and the computer software set some broad parameters for what might be done, and I'm sure the teachers are not loath to offer suggestions when students are stuck, intervene when chaos threatens, and so on. But by and large it is the students who set their agenda.

In the course of reaching their own goals, students inevitably develop and master certain skills and concepts, but mastery of skills and concepts that are designated as necessary or important by the teacher is not an educational aspiration of Papert's. What is most important for Papert is that students come to see themselves as capable of using knowledge to serve their *own* purposes.

Our concern at the moment, let's recall, is not with the attractiveness of Papert's educational vision but with the prospect that the computer will help usher in a megachange in the way children learn in school. It is clear to me that the way children learn in the Lego-Logo workshop is dramatically different from the way they learn in conventional classrooms. But the point to note here is that the workshop activity of children and teachers is intimately tied to a vision of education that is completely at variance with the conventional one. Here I want to note the difference between the role of the computer and that of the washing machine as catalysts for change. The washing machine accomplished with remarkable efficiency the *very same task* that housewives had engaged in so laboriously with corrugated washboards. No redefinition of the task was necessary for the benefits of the machine to become apparent. Still, so long as we stick to the conventional view of what teachers and students are sent to school for, we will view the Lego-Logo experience as diverting, entertaining, engaging, and motivating, but not as the kind of learning schools are designed to foster.

Papert is well aware of this. In answer to the question of why schools haven't witnessed dramatic changes in teaching and learning, he told an interviewer, " 'The educational establishment, including most of its research community, remains largely committed to the educational philosophy of the late 19th and early 20th centuries, and so far none of those who challenge these hallowed traditions has been able to loosen the hold of the educational establishment on how children are taught.' "[11]

The point I'm making is that computer technology will not loosen that hold by itself. Only those who already share Papert's iconoclastic view of what is important (a view that derives from the work of the Swiss psychologist Jean Piaget) will be very impressed with the blinking-light project. It is noteworthy here that Papert's laboratories are for the most part schools attended by children from poor backgrounds. Ironically, progressive educational views like Papert's are more likely to be found in highly educated, privileged environments, so that I would be surprised if Papert's success with Henry, Brian, and Maria would be the basis for mobilization by their parents and teachers on behalf of Papert's vision. Paradoxically, the computer's potential to be a catalyst for dramatic change in the role of the teacher depends on the machine's ability to outperform the teacher in his or her traditional role.

Barriers to Planned Change

For every story publicizing deplorable achievement results or conditions in schools, another story could be told trumpeting achievements and satisfied parents and students. Reform is difficult, in part because many students and teachers are relatively satisfied with the way things are. On the other hand, my guess is that if they were asked whether the American educational system needs to reform itself, the vast majority of citizens would likely say yes. Why, then, is reform so frustratingly difficult? One reason is that we are by no means agreed on the direction change should take. Rhetoric aiming at consensus for change often conceals substantially different priorities. Take the formulation of six educational goals for the year 2000 that the governors of the fifty states adopted in 1989 during the administration of President George Bush. One of the six goals was to raise the high school graduation rate to 90 percent (from about 75 percent). Another was to ensure that every American school is "free of drugs and violence."[12]

It takes no great insight to see that these two goals are in tension. If schools are to be drug- and violence-free, for example, students caught fighting or known to take or peddle drugs in school will have to be expelled, which is almost certain to *lower* the graduation rate, at least in the short run. Still another goal mandates that U.S. students "be first in the world in science and math achievement."[13] This vague statement presumably refers to the fact, among others, that a substantially higher percentage of young people in some other countries take a demanding math program that includes calculus. If we are to replicate their achievement, many more kids must master the math needed for access to calculus courses. Once again, at least in the short run, pursuit of this goal is almost certain to raise the failure rate in mathematics courses, making it more likely that some students will drop out before graduation.

Given the tension between worthy goals, how should we respond? Some might propose prioritizing them. Suppose we reach consensus that drug-free schools should be the first order of business, that raising graduation rates should be the focus of efforts only after schools are drug- and violence-free, and that mathematical achievement should be the third order of business. What would agreement on these priorities actually accomplish? First of all, the idea that the constituencies concerned with math achievement would just wait for the first two goals to be reached is ludicrous. It would not be long, indeed, before all those whose primary concern was one of the other five goals would be clamoring that their almost equally worthy goals were being held hostage to the war on drugs. The political forces arrayed against pursuing this one goal at the expense of the others would almost certainly prevail, and the decision to pursue the goals sequentially would be reversed.

Let's imagine for a moment, though, that we had only a single goal, to render our schools drug-free. That sounds simple enough. How might we accomplish it? I can easily imagine many citizens and educators lining up behind proposals for strengthening the power of police and school personnel to search students and students' lockers and to impose stiff penalties, leading quickly to suspension and expulsion, for students caught dealing or possessing drugs in school. Proponents would argue that our collective determination to stamp out such activities in school will be credible only if we send an unequivocal message about our refusal to tolerate them. Other parents and educators might favor an entirely different strategy: massive drug education and conflict-resolution programs in every grade along with counseling for students who succumb to drugs. Proponents of this strategy would point out to the first group that if the cost of keeping schools safe from drugs and violence is the creation of large gangs of drug- and violence-prone young people roaming the streets and shopping malls, it is a poor bargain. We can easily imagine additional arguments the proponents of each strategy would make. The point I'm trying to bring home is this: it is naive to think that if we could only achieve consensus on a goal, we could just move ahead without conflict to find the means of achieving it. All of the conflicts that were brushed under the rug in the effort to agree on the single most important goal would erupt during the process of attempting to agree on the means of reaching the goal.

It is as fallacious as it is seductive to believe that once we agree on the goals, once we agree, for example, on "what we want children to know and be able to do upon completion of their formal education, *other decisions begin to fall into place* [emphasis added]," to quote Chester Finn, Jr., former undersecretary of education.[14] This notion overlooks the fact that we can never achieve *only* the single state of affairs identified in the goal formulation. Depending on the means we adopt to reach the goal, a variety of states of affairs will come into existence. Since these other states of affairs, or side effects, often carry with them drastically different evaluations, it is no wonder that agreement on the goal may not reduce, much less eliminate, conflict.

Let me illustrate: consider once more the current, very justifiable, concern over school safety. Everyone may be presumed to want safe schools. But do we want safe schools and a police officer in every classroom? Do we want safe schools and a quarter of the juvenile population on the street or in prison? Do we want safe schools and a quarter of the juvenile population on tranquilizers? Do we want safe schools and half of each day's instructional time devoted to nonviolent conflict resolution? Do we want safe schools and a suspension of students' constitutional right to due process? Do we want safe schools and a counselor for every ten students? Of course, each choice involves not simply safe schools and some other single state of affairs, but innumerable changes that would have to be made to achieve that particular set of outcomes. I'm simplifying to illustrate the point that agreement on goals, even if we could get it, does *not* make other decisions "fall into place."

Thinking About Reform

School boards, administrators, and teachers are pushed and pulled in different directions by different constituencies with divergent agendas. One of the reasons our society pursues policies that are at cross-purposes with other policies, one of the reasons we sometimes see pendulum swings in the policies and stances adopted, is that, as I suggested above, many of the desirable qualities we'd like to see in schools are in tension with other desirable qualities we'd also like them to embody. For example, we'd like schools to offer a large array of activities utilizing the latest facilities, but we'd also like schools to be warm, familylike places that offer community and personal attention. We'd like schools to be places where children of high academic ability can mingle with those of limited ability, each group benefiting from acquaintance with the other, but we'd also like each child to be challenged and stretched to the limits of his or her academic ability, without needing to wait for classmates to catch up. We'd like a grading system in which grades have uniform, unequivocal meanings, but we'd also like a grading system in which children are not constantly compared with each other or made to feel superior or inferior to other children. We'd like children to develop a love for learning, yet we'd also like to assure ourselves that they know or can do certain things we designate as essential. We'd like athletic teams that give everyone a chance to participate and also win conference championships.

These tensions go beyond the inevitable struggles to satisfy multiple aspirations with limited resources, as in the desire to secure a high-quality science program *and* a high-quality music program. The aspirations I've identified above embody tensions that can't be reconciled through the infusion of additional funds. What should we do in the face of such tensions?

Part of the problem, I believe, may derive from the fact that we're accustomed to thinking of particular schools as good or bad or okay rather than as good for some purposes and bad for others. Consider the question of whether a particular model of automobile is a good car. Of course, we readily speak about good and bad cars, but we also speak about cars with respect to particular purposes. A vehicle may be good for commuting to work but bad for long trips; another may be good for showing off new wealth but bad for parking in tight spots; still another may be good for speed but bad for gasoline economy, or good for transporting a large family but bad for maneuvering in traffic. We all realize that when we buy an automobile, we must be prepared to make tradeoffs—a single car can't be all things to all people.

We don't seem to realize that the same thing is true with respect to schools. When school was less important, less was expected. Now many of us have expectations about schools that are not only much higher, but, so I'm arguing, mutually inconsistent. Where does this line of thinking lead us? It seems to me that it leads in the direction of diversifying our institutions, of trying to design schools that do some things very well while acknowledging that they fail at others.

If the movement for public choice maintains its current momentum, I would like to see parents and students able to choose between a variety of different schools, each of which would try to realize some excellent qualities at the expense of others. A large school might offer a highly diversified program and up-to-date equipment but not form as intimate a community as a much smaller school that prides itself on the way in which teachers get to know children as individuals. One school might offer all students a chance to participate on an athletic team if they wish to while another school, boasting of its outstanding record in interscholastic competition, necessarily limits participation to the most outstanding athletes. One school might have a grading system focused on a narrative discussion of students' developing competence, one that makes no comparisons between students, while another school might use a comparative grading system.

Such a diversity of institutions would begin to educate parents and citizens that with schools as with automobiles—they cannot be all things to all people. Such diversity is not inconsistent with some degree of uniformity. Consider automobiles again. All automobiles must meet gasoline mileage and safety standards. All public schools, likewise, would be required to meet the standards identified in Chapter Six—that they be open to public scrutiny and input and that they exclude no children on the basis of social background. Although I find this idea attractive, I recognize that it does carry the risk that ill-informed parental choices will limit children's educational futures. As with any new idea, it needs to be tried out first in a few school districts to see what the consequences are.

Reform in the Classroom

Ideas for reforming schools are many and various. I doubt that there are as many innovative ideas and actual reform projects under way in any other country. There's hardly an educational idea that hasn't been tried in some American school somewhere; nevertheless, many observers of goodwill are disappointed in the qualities of mind exhibited by the vast majority of teachers. Many of the reforms schools try to make don't penetrate into the classroom or, if they do, they don't really change the teaching patterns of the majority of teachers.

The stability of classroom patterns doesn't imply that they are well designed for the cultivation of the capacity and disposition to learn. Far from it. Many of these patterns appear natural enough to those of us who have never known anything different, but consider the response of Australian writer Jill Ker Conway to her first days in school at age eleven after life on an isolated sheep farm:

> I was used to knowing better than most people what needed to be done. Here I was the veriest incompetent, not only in games, but in the classroom, where there were also rules to be learned. It did no good to ask why the rules obtained. Answers were not forthcoming. One ruled the margin in one's book so; one set out mathematical exercises leaving two lines between calculations; one drew maps with a fine-tipped pen and India ink and in no other way. . . .
>
> The routines governing time were also puzzling. One just began studying one subject after everyone had been induced to sit still and be quiet, and suddenly a bell rang, the teacher departed, and we rushed into the gymnasium for an activity called physical exercise. . . . The purpose of all the activity was clear to everyone but me, and no explanations were ever given. . . . Because I read so much, I could excel at spelling bees. Our parents taught us to be the best at everything we did, but the things we were supposed to excel in had always before had some practical purpose. Now I was introduced to competition as an end in itself.[15]

It's indeed hard to believe that these patterns of school life are the best that humans can devise. Observers like Howard Gardner, who put prime emphasis on student understanding of the academic disciplines, argue that even our best students have a shallow understanding. Critics like Chester Finn, Jr., whose main criterion of schools' success is student mastery of factual knowledge, are equally disappointed. Those like myself, who consider the highest educational good to be the cultivation of certain capacities and dispositions, have no more reason to celebrate. Why doesn't the chorus of critical voices have more influence?

In my view, cultivation of children's dispositions and capacities is vital because it is these that determine what they will ultimately do as adults. But the same is true of teachers. Their patterns of activity are ultimately shaped by the dispositions they have developed. How have these dispositions been developed? Teachers' dispositions have been molded by literally thousands of hours of time spent observing the people who have taught them from first grade on through teacher training. Their students and their students' parents expect them to follow the familiar patterns as well. The textbooks they teach from reinforce those patterns. Even the organization of space and time in the classroom favors the traditional pedagogy. Is it any wonder that these patterns are so stable?

Even the changes that I've taken to be exemplars of dramatic transformation didn't happen all at once, but over a period of decades. How arrogant and naive of us to think that a few inspirational lectures, slide shows, books, journal articles, and summer workshops and a handful of new slogans and buzzwords could result in dramatic changes in patterns of activity that have been deeply etched into the fabric of schooling and into the psyches of all of us who are products of school.

How, then, can those of us who are committed to improving children's schooling avoid either despair or complacency? It is possible that over time new learning technologies will alter the familiar roles of teachers and students while leaving unchanged the traditional vision of education that is currently embodied in most computer-assisted learning. This is not the kind of megachange most reformers seek. Consider Seymour Papert's educational experiments again. I noted that the Lego-Logo classroom was an unlikely catalyst for reform, precisely because it depended on an altered vision of education that, although it is quite close to my own key aspirations, is difficult for many people to embrace. Nevertheless, unless alternative educational visions are realized in practice, they amount to no more than rhetoric. It is important, therefore, to maintain educational innovations such as Papert's and to challenge the idea that the success of such experiments should be judged by the standard criteria. History suggests that new technologies are not powerful enough by themselves to transform the familiar patterns of teaching and learning. And yet . . . if technologies for learning that embody alternative educational visions are sufficiently engaging, if they actually enhance children's capacity and propensity to learn, and if they provide a clear, new role for teachers, it is just barely possible that over the next several decades, the educational "cockroach" will find itself on the list of endangered species.

Chapter Nine

Summing Up

As I said at the outset, my primary aim in this work has not been to formulate and defend policy initiatives, but rather to examine and, hopefully, to change the perspective from which we view such initiatives. Too often, our ways of thinking in education are borrowed from highly focused pursuits such as business. Goals are formulated in terms of student attainment, means proposed for their accomplishment, tests devised to detect progress, and incentives structured to reward success and punish failure. Educators do disagree about which step should come first—restructuring the incentives, devising the tests, or getting consensus on the goals—yet too often the general approach goes unchallenged.

In my view, *the entire approach is misguided*. Educational reform is pointless if it does not change what people are disposed to do, what they can learn to do, and, most important, what they care about. A more knowledgeable cohort of young adults might enhance America's economic competitiveness, though there is room for doubt on that score, but a cohort committed to discovering and weighing evidence would enhance individual and collective well-being in myriad ways. Whether we're talking about teachers or students, changing what they deem important is hard, slow, frustrating work, made harder by a culture that transmits not a few negative messages about learning, especially school learning.

Keeping these aims in mind, we should not expect schools to change dramatically in a few years or even a few decades. Talk about redesigning or reinventing schools only sets us up for disappointment when the reforms don't pan out. A school's influence is wielded primarily by its teachers and even teachers cannot be expected to be immune to the disrespect for learning that infects parts of the larger culture. Although dramatic change in classrooms is unlikely, schools and school systems are far from stable, as I pointed out in the last chapter. The cumulative effect of relatively minor changes in educational policy over many years can make a significant difference. Although my reflections do not imply specific policy initiatives, I do offer some general guidance to practitioners and policy makers.

Almost everyone believes that the links between the school and the workplace need to be tightened; I argue, to the contrary, that they need to be loosened. We pride ourselves on our pluralism, our commitment to diversity, but we close all roads to a successful future that do not pass through at least twelve years of schooling. We tend to fool ourselves about the future demands of the workplace and the contribution of ever more schooling to human development. If young men and women decide not to go to college or, worse yet, to drop out of high school, we severely limit not only their own future opportunities but, indirectly, the opportunities of their children. The fact of the matter is that there will continue to be a very large number of jobs that require little expertise. Insisting that candidates for such jobs have ever higher levels of schooling leads only to alienation among the academically disinclined. If the resources of an affluent society were distributed more equally, if health care, paid vacations, and child care became entitlements, those entering low-paying occupations would face fewer barriers to a satisfying life.

What should schools teach? If the capacity and disposition to learn and the commitment to respect evidence are our central educational aspirations, we need to admit that conventional subject matter may not constitute the appropriate diet for all children at all times. Nevertheless, the experiments of progressive educators over the last hundred or so years do not give much comfort to those who think the conventional subjects should be eliminated. Alternative curricular diets look filling but don't provide the nutrients for long-term sustenance and growth. Almost all the important problems we face, individually and collectively, depend on the resources of more than a single discipline, yet without mastery of the disciplines themselves, those resources are simply unavailable. If we keep in mind what's truly important—enhancing children's propensity and capacity to learn—we may increase our willingness to experiment with different modes of curricular organization to find more balanced diets.

In my chapter on teaching, I argued that teaching is an activity woven into the fabric of our lives, yet exemplary teachers employ strategies that are far from instinctive. Teaching a class of children or adolescents well is an extremely difficult task; it is not one that is likely to be made easier by recent discoveries in the human sciences, or so I argue. Perhaps the main barrier to the improvement of teaching lies not in the technical or intellectual resources available to its practitioners, but in their work culture. Unlike most professionals, teachers work in isolation from peers and hence find it difficult to benefit from the observations and suggestions of those who've faced similar problems. The key to the improvement of teaching lies in the design of a more collaborative pedagogical culture in schools, one in which peers provide feedback to each other and share common concerns, one in which acknowledged master teachers work to improve the performance of novices. Moreover, those who teach specific subjects or specific student populations with distinctive needs and capacities must be encouraged to form collaborative networks across schools to benefit from each other's experience.

Developing a more collaborative work culture is, perhaps, the best way to enhance the commitment and performance of teachers and hence the best way to deal with the issue of accountability. The trend toward making teachers accountable for student performance on examinations needs to be halted, I argue. The "outcomes" approach to accountability distorts the educational process, focusing efforts on some children at the expense of others and overvaluing immediate goals at the expense of more important long-term aspirations.

Of course, public schools compete against other worthy uses of public funds, and it is entirely reasonable for citizens to demand and be provided with information about how their money is being spent. Education officials need to make more information available to the public about the policies that are in place and the extent to which they are actually followed. If schools and school systems are not complying with policies that are designed to enhance the educational experiences of students, the administrators and teachers who are responsible should be disciplined. The public does have a right to honest measures that indicate student academic achievement, but people need to understand that test scores, particularly those based on multiple-choice questions, don't capture what is most important in what schools do for children. Efforts must be directed at trying to find out how schools and teachers make a difference in fostering or impeding the development of the key dispositions that are of abiding value.

Teachers and schools should only be held accountable to the public if the public is the proper locus of educational authority. In Chapter Six, I pointed out that in the United States a traditional commitment to public education is in tension with the equally venerable idea that children's parents are the ultimate authorities in the educational sphere. I argued that the justification of public schools depends on two conditions: that such schools contain a mix of students representing diverse social and ethnic backgrounds and that the schools be receptive to input by parents and other citizens. In circumstances where schools fail to meet these requirements, their justification as public institutions is dubious. In order to merit continued support, public schools need to heed the voices of parents and citizens, and they need to exploit the diversity of their students for *educational* ends.

In Chapter Eight, I argued that one of the reasons for apparent pendulum swings in school reform is that our "ideal" school contains features that are not compatible with each other—a wealth of diverse learning opportunities and a small, familylike atmosphere, for example. I suggested that we learn to see schools, like automobiles, as good or bad *for certain purposes* rather than simply good or bad. This idea supports the creation of a more diverse set of public schools in which individual schools would feature different structures and educational philosophies, between which students and their parents would choose.

I agree with Seymour Papert that schooling does not exhibit the kind of megachange found in entertainment or medicine. But we need to ask, Are the megachanges in these fields associated with more certain, more durable, or less ambivalent satisfactions? The answer to this most important question is far from clear. These megachanges have been embraced precisely because they do not require a change in our commitment or our vision. But recently we have begun to question whether the revolutions in entertainment and medicine actually enhance the quality of our lives. The revolution in entertainment seems to leave many of us with our own capacities impoverished rather than enriched; the revolution in medicine leaves many of us confused about what we really should want from our health care providers. Megachange is tantamount to progress only when it is judged by the most superficial indicators.

What ought to be central to the educational mission, I've argued, is concern with developing in students a respect for evidence and supporting growth in students' capacity and desire to keep on learning. This requires a change that can only be slow and gradual, a change in the kind of culture we have created. My message is not intended to be a counsel of despair, still less an excuse for inaction. As I said in Chapter Four, regardless of whether we have the *job* of teaching school, most of us teach much more than we realize. By keeping our own curiosity alive, by showing our own respect for evidence and argument, we each add our own small but meaningful effort to demonstrate and hence to teach the next generation that these are matters we truly care about.

Notes

Chapter One: Why Philosophy?

1. On the influence of Dewey and progressive education, see L. Cuban, *How Teachers Taught: Constancy and Change in American Classrooms* (White Plains, N.Y.: Longman, 1984); H. M. Kliebard, *The Struggle for the American Curriculum 1893–1958* (New York: Routledge, 1986). Dewey's most complete treatise on education is *Democracy and Education* (New York: Macmillan, 1916). An excellent intellectual biography of Dewey is R. B. Westbrook, *John Dewey and American Democracy* (Ithaca, N.Y.: Cornell University Press, 1991).
2. L. Olson, "Eleven Design Teams Are Tapped to Pursue Their Visions of 'Break the Mold' Schools," *Education Week*, Aug. 5, 1992, pp. 1, 47–52.

Chapter Two: Aspirations

1. D. T. Kearns and D. P. Doyle, *Winning the Brain Race: A Bold Plan to Make Our Schools Competitive* (San Francisco: ICS Press, 1988); E. D. Hirsch, Jr., *Cultural Literacy: What Every American Needs to Know* (Boston: Houghton Mifflin, 1987); C. E. Finn, Jr., "A Nation Still at Risk," *Commentary*, May 1987, pp. 17–23; W. J. Bennett, *James Madison High School: A Curriculum for American Students* (Washington, D.C.: U.S. Department of Education, 1987); H. Gardner, *The Unschooled Mind: How Children Think and How Schools Should Teach* (New York: Basic Books, 1991).

2. W. G. Spady, "Organizing for Results: The Basis of Authentic Restructuring and Reform," *Educational Leadership*, 1988, 46(2), 4–8.

3. R. Kelly, review of *Life Work* by Donald Hall, *New York Times Book Review*, Oct. 1993, p. 11.

4. J. Rawls, *A Theory of Justice* (Cambridge, Mass.: Harvard University Press, 1971), pp. 17–22.

5. An excellent recent discussion of student assessment is found in G. P. Wiggins, *Assessing Student Performance: Exploring the Purpose and Limits of Testing* (San Francisco: Jossey-Bass, 1993). It is interesting that in the authoritative account of Dewey's own laboratory school at the University of Chicago, written by two of its teachers, there is no mention of student evaluation whatever. See K. C. Mayhew and A. C. Edwards, *The Dewey School: The Laboratory School of the University of Chicago, 1893–1903* (New York: Atherton Press, 1965; originally published 1936).

Chapter Three: Curriculum

1. The arguments with regard to the nineteenth century are reviewed in J. Spring, *The American School 1642–1993* (3rd ed.) (New York: McGraw Hill, 1994), pp. 86–94; pp. 235–242 review the debate for the early twentieth century.

2. I did not invent these illustrations. They are all projects that schools have actually carried out, according to accounts I have read or people I've spoken to.

3. S. Papert, *The Children's Machine: Rethinking School in the Age of the Computer* (New York: Basic Books, 1993), pp. 116–124.

4. M. Oakeshott, "A Place of Learning," in T. Fuller (ed.), *The Voice of Liberal Learning: Michael Oakeshott on Education* (New Haven, Conn.: Yale University Press, 1989; originally published 1975), pp. 36–39.

Chapter Four: Teaching

1. N. Oxenhandler, "La Bourdonneuse," *New Yorker*, May 10, 1993, p. 39.

2. J. T. Bruer, "The Mind's Journey from Novice to Expert," *American Educator*, 1993, *17*(2), 6–15, 38–46.

3. Bruer, "The Mind's Journey," p. 43.

4. Bruer, "The Mind's Journey," p. 43.

5. Bruer, "The Mind's Journey," p. 43.

6. Bruer, "The Mind's Journey," p. 43.

7. Bruer, "The Mind's Journey," p. 43.

8. J. E. Brophy and T. L. Good, "Teacher Behavior and Student Achievement," in M. C. Wittrock (ed.), *Handbook of Research on Teaching* (3rd ed.) (New York: Macmillan, 1986), p. 366.

9. Brophy and Good, "Teacher Behavior," p. 366.

10. Bruer, "The Mind's Journey," p. 45.

11. Bruer, "The Mind's Journey," pp.7–8.

12. See A. Palincsar and A. Brown, "Reciprocal Teaching of Comprehension-Fostering and Monitoring Activities," *Cognition and Instruction*, 1984, *1*(2), 117–175.

13. Bruer, "The Mind's Journey," p. 40.

14. Bruer, "The Mind's Journey," p. 41.

15. "Penicillin," in R. E. McGrew (ed.), *Encyclopedia of Medical History* (London: Macmillan, 1985), p. 248.

16. J. W. Popham and E. Baker, *Systematic Instruction* (Englewood Cliffs, N.J.: Prentice-Hall, 1970), pp. 19-20, emphasis in original.

17. Popham and Baker, *Systematic Instruction*, p. 20.

18. Bruer, "The Mind's Journey," p. 7.

19. My colleague Herbert Kliebard first brought this analogy to my attention.

20. Oxenhandler, "La Bourdonneuse," p. 39.

21. Oxenhandler, "La Bourdonneuse," p. 40.

22. There are many worthwhile discussions of teaching. For the reader interested in pursuing the subject, I'd recommend starting with P. W. Jackson, *The Practice of Teaching* (New York: Teachers College Press, 1986).

Chapter Five: Accountability

1. O. Johnson (ed.), *Information Please Almanac* (47th ed.) (Boston: Houghton Mifflin, 1994), pp. 713–719.

2. "Westinghouse Science Search Names 40 Student Finalists," *New York Times*, Jan. 24, 1994, National edition, sec. A, p. 7. A comprehensive review of the state of American public schools that comes to a decidedly positive conclusion may be found in G. W. Bracey, "The Third Bracey Report on the Condition of Public Education," *Phi Delta Kappan*, 1993, *75*(2), 104–117.

3. D. A. Archbald and F. M. Newmann, *Beyond Standardized Testing: Assessing Authentic Academic Achievement in the Secondary School* (Reston, Va.: National Association of Secondary School Principals, 1988), p. 16.

4. J. E. Brophy and T. L. Good, "Teacher Behavior and Student Achievement," in M. C. Wittrock (ed.), *Handbook of Research on Teaching* (3d ed.) (New York: Macmillan, 1986), p. 366, emphasis mine.

5. R. Rothman, "Study Urges 'Learning Communities' to Address the Isolation of Teachers," *Education Week*, Mar. 17, 1993, pp. 1, 25. James Stigler and Harold Stevenson report that elementary teachers in Japan often work on lesson plans jointly and critique each other's lessons. See J. W. Stigler and H. W. Stevenson, "How Asian Teachers Polish Each Lesson to Perfection," *American Educator*, 1991, *15*(4), 46.

6. T. Sowell, *Inside American Education: The Decline, the Deception, the Dogmas* (New York: Macmillan, 1993), p. 12.

7. R. Rothman, "Ky. Reformers Await Reaction to Results of Tough New Tests," *Education Week*, Sep. 23, 1993, pp. 1, 20. For a fuller account of the Kentucky reform initiative, see B. E. Steffy, *The Kentucky Education Reform: Lessons for America* (Lancaster, Pa.: Technomic, 1993).

8. Sowell, *Inside American Education*, p. 8.

9. W. Celis III, "School-Management Company Admits Overstating Test Gains," *New York Times*, June 8, 1994, National edition, sec. C, p. 18.

10. S. M. Elam, L. C. Rose, and A. M. Gallup, "Phi Delta Kappa/Gallup Poll of the Public's Attitudes Toward the Public Schools," *Phi Delta Kappan*, 1993, *75*(2), 138.

11. National Center for Education Statistics, *Digest of Education Statistics 1992* (Washington, D.C.: U.S. Department of Education, Oct. 1992), Table 157, p. 160.

Chapter Six: Authority

1. L. Lomasky, *Persons, Rights, and the Moral Community* (New York: Oxford University Press, 1987), p. 175. For a contrasting view, the reader might try A. Gutmann's *Democratic Education* (Princeton, N.J.: Princeton University Press, 1987).
2. Lomasky, *Persons*, p. 26.
3. B. Rush, *Essays, Literary, Moral and Philosophical* (2d ed.) (Philadelphia: T. and W. Bradford, 1806), pp. 6–7, cited in K. Alexander, "Equity, Equality, and the Common Good in Educational Financing," in D. Verstegen and J. G. Ward (eds.), *Spheres of Justice in Education: Eleventh Annual Yearbook of the American Education Finance Association* (New York: HarperBusiness, 1991), p. 270.
4. A. Bradley, "'Strong Democracy' Yields Improvement in Chicago Reforms," *Education Week*, July 14, 1993, p. 1.
5. See M. Walsh, "Wisconsin Court Upholds State's Test of Vouchers," *Education Week*, Mar. 11, 1992, pp. 1, 27.
6. *Statistical Abstract of the United States 1992* (112th ed.) (Washington, D.C.: U.S. Department of Commerce, 1993), p. 20.
7. J. Moline, "Teachers and Professionalism," in C. E. Finn, Jr., D. Ravitch, and R. T. Fancher (eds.), *Against Mediocrity: The Humanities in America's High Schools* (New York: Holmes & Meier, 1984), p. 206, emphasis in original.
8. Moline, "Teachers and Professionalism," pp. 205–206.
9. Moline, "Teachers and Professionalism," p. 204.
10. R. P. Doyle, "The Resistance of Conventional Wisdom to Research Evidence: The Case of Retention in Grade," *Phi Delta Kappan*, 1989, *71*(3), 215–220.

Chapter Seven: Inequalities

1. S. Greenhouse, "Clinton Seeks to Narrow a Growing Wage Gap," *New York Times*, Dec. 13, 1993, National edition, sec. C, p. 1.

2. L. Thurow, *Head to Head: The Coming Economic Battle Among Japan, Europe, and America* (New York: Warner Books, 1992), p. 164.

3. B. D. Whitehead, "Dan Quayle Was Right," *Atlantic*, Apr. 1993, p. 62.

4. Whitehead, "Dan Quayle," p. 47.

5. L. Mishel and D. M. Frankel, *The State of Working America* (1990–91 ed.) (Armonk, N.Y.: M.E. Sharpe, 1991), p. 7.

6. H. Hodgkinson, "Reform Versus Reality," in F. Schultz (ed.), *Education 93/94* (Guilford, Conn.: Dushkin Publishing Group, 1993), p. 39.

7. Mishel and Frankel, *The State of Working America*, p. 171.

8. W. Celis III, "Study Finds Rising Concentration of Black and Hispanic Students," *New York Times*, Dec. 14, 1993, National edition, sec. A, pp. 1, 11.

9. "The New Face of America," *Time*, Special Issue, Fall 1993, p. 14.

10. "The New Face of America," p. 14.

11. National Center for Education Statistics, *Digest of Education Statistics 1992* (Washington, D.C.: U.S. Department of Education, Oct. 1992), Table 157, p. 159.

12. Hodgkinson, "Reform Versus Reality," p. 40.

13. L. V. Hedges, R. D. Laine, and R. Greenwald, "Does Money Matter? A Meta-Analysis of Studies of the Effects of Differential School Inputs on Student Outcomes," *Educational Researcher*, 1994, *23*(3), 5–14.

14. Mishel and Frankel, *The State of Working America*, p. 260; T. M. Smeeding, "Why the U.S. Antipoverty System Doesn't Work Very Well," *Challenge*, 1992, *35*(1), 31. The poverty rate is here defined as the percentage of people below 40 percent of adusted median family income after tax and transfer. The seven are Canada, Australia, Sweden, Germany, the Netherlands, France, and the United Kingdom.

15. See C. Jencks, *Inequality: A Reassessment of the Effect of Family and Schooling in America* (New York: Basic Books, 1972), chap. 7, "Income Inequality," pp. 209–246.

16. P. Schmidt, "La Crosse to Push Ahead with Income-Based Busing Plan," *Education Week*, Aug. 5, 1992, p. 10; and P. Schmidt, "Five on Wausau Board Voted Out over Busing Stands," *Education Week*, Jan. 12, 1994, p. 5.

17. Thurow, *Head to Head*, p. 138.

18. "What CEO's Make," *Fortune*, June 1993, p. 103.

19. J. M. Berman and T. Cosca, "The 1990–2005 Job Outlook in Brief," *Occupational Outlook Quarterly*, 1992, *36*(1), 17, 30.

20. P. T. Kilborn, "For High School Graduates, a Job Market of Dead Ends," *New York Times*, May 30, 1994, National edition, sec. A, pp. 1, 26.

21. M. Csikszentmihalyi, "Contexts of Optimal Growth in Childhood," *Daedalus*, 1993, *122*(1), 47.

22. Csikszentmihalyi, "Contexts," p. 48.

23. C. E. Finn, Jr., *We Must Take Charge: Our Schools and Our Future* (New York: Free Press, 1992), p. 253.

24. J. A. O'Day and M. S. Smith, "Systemic Reform and Educational Opportunity," in S. H. Fuhrman (ed.), *Designing Coherent Education Policy: Improving the System* (San Francisco: Jossey-Bass, 1993), p. 265, emphasis in original.

25. Finn, *We Must Take Charge*, p. 254.

26. W. Stegner, *Where the Bluebird Sings to the Lemonade Springs: Living and Writing in the West* (New York: Penguin Books, 1992), p. 104.

27. J. Gross, "To Help Girls Keep Up, Girls-Only Math Classes," *New York Times*, Nov. 24, 1993, National edition, sec. A, p. 1.

Chapter Eight: Change

1. I borrow this label from David Tyack, who uses it in a similar way in "Public School Reform: Policy Talk and Institutional Practice," *American Journal of Education*, 1991, *100*(1), 1–19.

2. S. Papert, *The Children's Machine: Rethinking School in the Age of the Computer* (New York: Basic Books, 1993); on the microeconomy school, see G. Richmond, "The Future School: Is

Lowell Pointing Us Toward a Revolution in Education?" *Phi Delta Kappan*, 1989, 71(3), 232–236. Founded in 1974, the Future Problem Solving Program involves students from grades four through twelve in attempting to solve complex scientific and social problems. Working in teams of four, the students compete against teams from other schools in their own state and around the country.

3. See R. S. Cowan, *More Work for Mother: The Ironies of Household Technology from the Open Hearth to the Microwave* (New York: Basic Books, 1983); and N. Du Vall, *Domestic Technology: A Chronology of Developments* (Boston: Hall, 1988).

4. See H. Sitkoff, *The Struggle for Black Equality 1954–1980* (New York: Hill and Wang, 1981).

5. Papert, *The Children's Machine*, p. 6.

6. The invention of the calculator might have been expected to revolutionize the teaching of arithmetic, but it hasn't. Educators are still in disagreement about how to assimilate it.

7. Papert, *The Children's Machine*, p.47.

8. Papert, *The Children's Machine*, pp. 116–125.

9. Papert, *The Children's Machine*, p. 123.

10. Papert, *The Children's Machine*, pp. 123–124.

11. D. Hill, "Inventing the Future," *Education Week*, Jan. 12, 1994, p. 36.

12. R. Rothman, "1st Goals Report Contains Failures and Incompletes," *Education Week*, Oct. 2, 1991, p. 18.

13. Rothman, "1st Goals Report," p. 18.

14. C. E. Finn, Jr., *We Must Take Charge: Our Schools and Our Future* (New York: Free Press, 1992), p. 251.

15. J. K. Conway, *The Road from Coorain* (New York: Vintage Books, 1989), pp. 87–88.

Bibliography

Alexander, K. "Equity, Equality, and the Common Good in Educational Financing." In D. Verstegen and J. G. Ward (eds.), *Spheres of Justice in Education: Eleventh Annual Yearbook of the American Education Finance Association* (pp. 269–294). New York: HarperBusiness, 1991.

Archbald, D. A., and Newmann, F. M. *Beyond Standardized Testing: Assessing Authentic Academic Achievement in the Secondary School.* Reston, Va.: National Association of Secondary School Principals, 1988.

Bennett, W. J. *James Madison High School: A Curriculum for American Students.* Washington, D.C.: U.S. Department of Education, 1987.

Berman, J. M., and Cosca, T. "The 1990–2005 Job Outlook in Brief." *Occupational Outlook Quarterly,* 1992, *36*(1), 6–41.

Bracey, G. W. "The Third Bracey Report on the Condition of Public Education." *Phi Delta Kappan,* 1993, *75*(2), 104–117.

Bradley, A. "'Strong Democracy' Yields Improvement in Chicago Reforms." *Education Week,* July 14, 1993, pp. 1,13.

Brophy, J. E., and Good, T. L. "Teacher Behavior and Student Achievement." In M. L. Wittrock (ed.), *Handbook of Research on Teaching.* (3rd ed., pp. 328–375.) New York: Macmillan, 1986.

Bruer, J. T. "The Mind's Journey from Novice to Expert." *American Educator,* 1993, *17*(2), 6–15, 38–46.

Celis III, W. "Study Finds Rising Concentration of Black and Hispanic Students." *New York Times,* Dec. 14, 1993, National edition, sec. A, pp. 1, 11.

Celis III, W. "School-Management Company Admits Overstating Test Gains." *New York Times,* June 8, 1994, National edition, sec. C, p. 18.

Conway, J. K. *The Road from Coorain.* New York: Vintage Books, 1989.

Cowan, R. S. *More Work for Mother: The Ironies of Household Technology from the Open Hearth to the Microwave.* New York: Basic Books, 1983.

Csikszentmihalyi, M. "Contexts of Optimal Growth in Childhood." *Daedalus,* 1993, *122*(1), 31–56.

Cuban, L. *How Teachers Taught: Constancy and Change in American Classrooms.* White Plains, N.Y.: Longman, 1984.

Dewey, J. *Democracy and Education.* New York: Macmillan, 1916.

Dewey, J. *Experience and Education*. New York: Macmillan, 1938.

Doyle, R. P. "The Resistance of Conventional Wisdom to Research Evidence: The Case of Retention in Grade." *Phi Delta Kappan*, 1989, 71(3), 215–220.

Du Vall, N. *Domestic Technology: A Chronology of Developments*. Boston: Hall, 1988.

Elam, S. M., Rose, L. C., and Gallup, A. M. "Phi Delta Kappa/Gallup Poll of the Public's Attitudes Toward the Public Schools." *Phi Delta Kappan*, 1993, 75(2), 138–157.

Finn, C. E., Jr. "A Nation Still at Risk." *Commentary*, May 1987, pp. 17–23.

Finn, C. E., Jr. *We Must Take Charge: Our Schools and Our Future*. New York: Free Press, 1992.

Gardner, H. *The Unschooled Mind: How Children Think and How Schools Should Teach*. New York: Basic Books, 1991.

Gross, J. "To Help Girls Keep Up, Girls-Only Math Classes." *New York Times*, Nov. 24, 1993, National edition, sec. A, p. 1.

Gutmann, A. *Democratic Education*. Princeton, N.J.: Princeton University Press, 1987.

Hedges, L. V., Laine, R. D., and Greenwald, R. "Does Money Matter? A Meta-Analysis of Studies of the Effects of Differential School Inputs on Student Outcomes." *Educational Researcher*, 1994, 23(3), 5–14.

Hill, D. "Inventing the Future." *Education Week*, Jan. 12, 1994, pp. 36–39.

Hirsch, E. D., Jr. *Cultural Literacy: What Every American Needs to Know*. Boston: Houghton Mifflin, 1987.

Hodgkinson, H. "Reform Versus Reality." In F. Schultz (ed.), *Education 93/94* (pp. 36–42). Guilford, Conn.: Dushkin Publishing Group, 1993.

Jackson, P. W. *The Practice of Teaching*. New York: Teachers College Press, 1986.

Jencks, C. *Inequality: A Reassessment of the Effect of Family and Schooling in America*. New York: Basic Books, 1972.

Johnson, O. (ed.). *Information Please Almanac*. (47th ed.) Boston: Houghton Mifflin, 1994.

Kearns, D. T., and Doyle, D. P. *Winning the Brain Race: A Bold Plan to Make Our Schools Competitive*. San Francisco: ICS Press, 1988.

Kelly, R. Review of *Life Work* by Donald Hall. *New York Times Book Review*, Oct. 3, 1993, p. 11.

Kilborn, P. T. "For High School Graduates, a Job Market of Dead Ends." *New York Times*, May 30, 1994, National edition, sec. A, pp. 1, 26.

Kliebard, Herbert M. *The Struggle for the American Curriculum 1893–1958*. New York: Routledge, 1986.

Lomasky, L. *Persons, Rights, and the Moral Community*. New York: Oxford University Press, 1987.

McGrew, R. E. (ed.). *Encyclopedia of Medical History*. London: Macmillan, 1985.

Mayhew, K. C., and Edwards, A. C. *The Dewey School: The Laboratory School of the University of Chicago, 1893–1903*. New York: Atherton Press, 1965. (Originally published 1936.)

Mishel, L., and Frankel, D. M. *The State of Working America*. (1990–91 ed.) Armonk, N.Y.: M. E. Sharpe, 1991.

Moline, J. "Teachers and Professionalism." In C. E. Finn, Jr., D. Ravitch, and R. T. Fancher (eds.), *Against Mediocrity: The Humanities in America's High Schools* (pp. 197–213). New York: Holmes & Meier, 1984.

National Center for Education Statistics. *Digest of Education Statistics 1992*. Washington, D.C.: U.S. Department of Education, Oct. 1992.

Newell, A., and Simon, H. A. *Human Problem Solving*. Englewood Cliffs, N.J.: Prentice-Hall, 1972.

Oakeshott, M. "A Place of Learning." In T. Fuller (ed.), *The Voice of Liberal Learning: Michael Oakeshott on Education* (pp. 17–42). New Haven, Conn.: Yale University Press, 1989. (Originally published 1975.)

O'Day, J. A., and Smith, M. S. "Systemic Reform and Educational Opportunity." In S. H. Fuhrman (ed.), *Designing Coherent Education Policy: Improving the System* (pp. 250–312). San Francisco: Jossey-Bass, 1993.

Olson, L. "Eleven Design Teams Are Tapped to Pursue Their Visions of 'Break the Mold' Schools." *Education Week*, Aug. 5, 1992, pp. 1, 47–52.

Oxenhandler, N. "La Bourdonneuse." *New Yorker*, May 10, 1993, pp. 39–40.

Palincsar, A., and Brown, A. "Reciprocal Teaching of Comprehension-Fostering and Monitoring Activities." *Cognition and Instruction*, 1984, *1*(2), 117–175.

Papert, S. *The Children's Machine: Rethinking School in the Age of the Computer*. New York: Basic Books, 1993.

Popham, W. J., and Baker, E. *Systematic Instruction*. Englewood Cliffs, N.J.: Prentice-Hall, 1970.

Rawls, J. *A Theory of Justice*. Cambridge, Mass.: Harvard University Press, 1971.

Richmond, G. "The Future School: Is Lowell Pointing Us Toward a Revolution in Education?" *Phi Delta Kappan*, 1989, *71*(3), 232–236.

Rothman, R. "1st Goals Report Contains Failures and Incompletes." *Education Week*, Oct. 2, 1991, p. 18.

Rothman, R. "Ky. Reformers Await Reaction to Results of Tough New Tests." *Education Week*, Sep. 23, 1992, pp. 1, 20.

Rothman, R. "Study Urges 'Learning Communities' to Address the Isolation of Teachers." *Education Week*, Mar. 17, 1993, pp. 1, 25.

Rush, B. *Essays, Literary, Moral and Philosophical*. (2d ed.) Philadelphia: T. and W. Bradford, 1806.

Schmidt, P. "La Crosse to Push Ahead with Income-Based Busing Plan." *Education Week*, Aug. 5, 1992, p. 10.

Schmidt, P. "Five on Wausau Board Voted Out over Busing Stands." *Education Week*, Jan. 12, 1994, p. 5.

Sitkoff, H. *The Struggle for Black Equality 1954–1980.* New York: Hill and Wang, 1981.

Smeeding, T. M. "Why the U.S. Antipoverty System Doesn't Work Very Well." *Challenge,* 1992, *35*(1), 30–35.

Sowell, T. *Inside American Education: The Decline, the Deception, the Dogmas.* New York: Macmillan, 1993.

Spady, W. G. "Organizing for Results: The Basis of Authentic Restructuring and Reform." *Educational Leadership,* 1988, *46*(2), 4–8.

Spring, J. *The American School 1642–1993.* (3rd ed.) New York: McGraw-Hill, 1994.

Steffy, B. E. *The Kentucky Education Reform: Lessons for America.* Lancaster, Pa.: Technomic, 1993.

Stegner, W. *Where the Bluebird Sings to the Lemonade Springs: Living and Writing in the West.* New York: Penguin Books, 1992.

Stigler, J. W., and Stevenson, H. W. "How Asian Teachers Polish Each Lesson to Perfection." *American Educator,* 1991, *15*(4), 12–20, 43–47.

Thurow, L. *Head to Head: The Coming Economic Battle Among Japan, Europe, and America.* New York: Warner Books, 1992.

Tyack, D. "Public School Reform: Policy Talk and Institutional Practice." *American Journal of Education,* 1991, *100*(1), 1–19.

Walsh, M. "Wisconsin Court Upholds State's Test of Vouchers." *Education Week,* Mar. 11, 1992, pp. 1, 27.

Westbrook, R. B. *John Dewey and American Democracy.* Ithaca, N.Y.: Cornell University Press, 1991.

Whitehead, B. D. "Dan Quayle Was Right." *Atlantic,* Apr. 1993, pp. 47–84.

Wiggins, G. P. *Assessing Student Performance: Exploring the Purpose and Limits of Testing.* San Francisco: Jossey-Bass, 1993.

Index

The Author

Francis Schrag is professor and chair of the Department of Educational Policy Studies and professor of philosophy at the University of Wisconsin, Madison. He earned his B.A. degree (1959) from Cornell University in philosophy and his Ed.D. degree (1970) from Teachers College, Columbia University, in philosophy of education. Before joining the faculty at Wisconsin, he taught at the University of Chicago for three years.

Schrag's scholarly interests have ranged widely in philosophy of education, ethics, social philosophy, and philosophy of the social sciences. His articles have appeared in a variety of educational and philosophical journals, including, among others, the *American Journal of Education*, *Educational Theory*, *Educational Researcher*, *Philosophy*, *Inquiry*, and *Political Theory*. A previous book, *Thinking in School and Society*, was published in 1988.